# Mommy Divas on the Move

## 16 SUCCESSFUL SECRETS FOR MOMPRENEURS

*Patrice Tartt*

*Mommy Divas on the Move: 16 Successful Secrets for Mompreneurs*
© 2014 by Patrice Tartt
Patrice Tartt Publishing, LLC
www.patricetartt.com

ISBN-13: 978-0615994215
ISBN-10: 0615994210
Library of Congress Control Number: 2014915767
Patrice Tartt, Woodbridge, VA

Please visit the Mommy Divas on the Move website and social media pages to stay connected and updated on events and upcoming projects and to purchase additional copies:

www.MommyDivasOnTheMove.com

Twitter.com/MommyDivasOTM
Facebook.com/MommyDivasOnTheMove
Instagram: MommyDivasOnTheMove

For more information on the author, please visit her website and social media pages to stay connected and updated on new projects:

www.PatriceTartt.com

Twitter.com/PatriceTartt
Facebook.com/PatriceTartt
Instagram: PatriceTartt

If you are interested in a partnership with Mommy Divas on the Move, LLC or interested in becoming a GLAMbassador, please visit the MDOTM website for more information.

# Dedication

*I dedicate this book to my handsome and lovable son Bron Jaden, who is the JOY of my life and the reason I am a mommy, and to my mother for raising a diva. She is the Queen Mommy Diva, so I learned from the BEST. Last but not least, to my dad, you are the reason that I write. You are truly missed and will never be forgotten. R.I.P.*

*I love you all!*

# *Acknowledgements*

Writing takes a lot of time and dedication. I couldn't have completed this project without my main supporters. I would like to take this time to thank the following individuals:

To my mother Elaine Tartt and bestie Danielle Joyce for always being supportive and encouraging me along the way with your kind words. Thank you and I love you both.

A special thanks to Zelda Corona for all of your hard work and assisting me with this project. You are my ace boon!

To all of my family and friends, I thank you as well for believing in me.

To my wonderful contributors, thank you for trusting me to bring my vision to fruition and for your contributions to this phenomenal project. We did it!

# Table of Contents

# Foreword

# MIA REDRICK

## The Mom Strategist™

Supporting moms in both their life and business from all walks of life to discover and realize their greatest goals is my life's work. Making the decision to become a mompreneur is an important one. It means that you will learn more about your fears, strengths, network, tribe, and the resources that you need to save time, money and energy than you ever have in your life. It means that you will take control of your financial destiny. When I started my business nine years ago, I remember trying to carefully balance my role as mom, wife, CEO, sales support, cook, carpooler, and so many other roles that I was playing in my life. It took time, patience, mentors, coaches, and other mompreneurs to teach me that I could honor my desire to be a great business owner and still rock motherhood.

*Mommy Divas on the Move: 16 Successful Secrets for Mompreneurs* shares the successes and the struggles of being a mom in business. My failures have laid the foundation for my greatest lessons and success. Ask any successful business owner her secrets to becoming successful, and she will likely say being fearless, taking action, making bold requests of yourself, networking up, creating a team to support your vision, setting boundaries, and delegating. Women need and want to know that the path to accomplishing their dreams in both their business and in their life is possible.

The stories contained in this book provide the roadmap for all mom entrepreneurs who want to learn from women managing motherhood and entrepreneurship. We want to know the secrets to overcoming the common obstacles of motherhood like unscheduled interruptions, finding time to balance life and work, and the secrets to staying focused.

I have always thought that a book that talks about the real struggles and strategies to excel in both business and in life for mothers needed to be written. This book answers all of our unanswered questions, and by such a diverse group of mothers.

The contributors in this book represent many aspects of motherhood including single, married, divorced, widowed, mom to children with special needs, bonus moms, and moms of young children to adults. Each of them has shared their greatest challenges and how they have overcome those obstacles to accomplish their dreams. This book is a blueprint for all mothers who want to know how they can make their dreams take flight and want to know how other women have done the same with their circumstances.

When mothers hear the authentic struggles of other women as well as the personal growth and changes that they had to make to become successful, it inspires everyone and lets each of us know that our highest visions are possible. When I started my business there were no formulas to becoming a successful mom coach. I wanted to know how I could build a successful and profitable business that would allow me to be the type of mom and wife I desired without comprising my lifestyle. I did not want my success to be at the expense of having a great marriage and being an available mother. I desperately needed a tool like this book to validate me and let me know that I was not alone.

Along the way, I met amazing mentors and coaches who told me that understanding my own definition of success would serve me the most as I created the systems for both my business and in my life. I learned that I never desired to be a "supermom" but instead wanted to be a super mom to my children, and that meant learning how to do less well. Yes, I learned through trial and error that the key to my success was understanding the resources that supported my growth, the boundaries to maintain my sanity, and taking action during the key windows of opportunity. As a result, I have grown a brand that has touched millions every week as The Mom Strategist™ on the Emmy nominated show America Now. My books have become bestsellers and my Time for Mom-me™ system has changed the lives of tens of thousands of women in partnership with national brands like Panera Bread Corporation, Great Harvest Bread Company and Corner Bakery Café' nationwide as well as in Australia. My challenge to solve the greatest struggle in motherhood called work/life satisfaction, has allowed me to touch millions around the world.

This book is for every mom entrepreneur who knows that she has a dream calling her and that she wants to monetize it. It might be an idea that only you see for now that you want to birth, or it might be a conventional business or service that we have grown to know and love. I want you to know that you can do it! You can have success if you create a plan and work it. If you feed your mind and soul with resources like *Mommy Divas on the Move: 16 Successful Secrets for Mompreneurs* that will give you the inspiration, practical steps, strategies and encouragement, from moms who have done it already.

I encourage you to find your passion and dare to live it every day. Brava to Patrice Tartt for assembling a mom entrepreneurial dream team.

# Introduction

# PATRICE TARTT

## Chief Mommy Diva

Where do I begin? Let me reminisce for a minute back to the conception of *Mommy Divas on the Move: 16 Successful Secrets for Mompreneurs*. Fall of 2013 allowed me to plunge further into my purpose and align myself right where God needed me to be to birth this concept, this book, this Mommy Divas on the Move-ment. My mind is literally a think tank, a breeding ground for concepts and anything else that will allow me to further my purpose in the world while on this journey called "Life" to my destiny.

As a mom, I knew there had to be more to life than just working a nine-to-five, being stuck in morning *and* evening DC traffic, rushing to pick up my little one from daycare, getting him fed, and only spending a few hours with him before his bedtime. Then I would have to do it all over again the very next day. I also knew I wasn't the only mom who eventually wanted to make the transition from being a full-time employee to being fully self-employed, or the mom who wanted to start her own business but needed a better understanding of the highs and lows of being a mompreneur. Let's not forget the mom who was already a mompreneur but needed additional inspiration when the lows outweighed the highs. There had to be some type of magical guide, not only to inspire, that all mompreneurs could relate to regardless of their marital status. You know, like the guide you get in the mail after you have a baby called *Parenting 101*, NOT! My favorite quote of all time is by the phenomenal author Toni Morrison: *If there's a book* you *really want to read, but it hasn't been written yet, then* you *must write it.*

That was it! I had to write it and not by myself. I needed other mompreneurs to join me as contributors in order to get other perspectives on mompreneurship. Initially, I never imagined *Mommy Divas on the Move* being anything other than a book, and I envisioned only having enough contributors that I could count on one hand and those being mompreneurs who I already knew. I never imagined in my wildest dreams it would take off like wildfire and that the concept of what a mommy diva is would resonate with so many women. I am truly amazed at God's favor and all the things he has done for me concerning this project and what he continues to do on a daily basis.

Sixteen women later and after many sleepless, long nights and days stressing that I wouldn't be able to pull everything off, I'm a one-woman band. Well, I'm a solopreneur at least until my book is on Oprah's coffee table and I'm invited to do a Super Soul Sunday segment with the queen of talk. I implore every mompreneur, whether she is seasoned in her business or just now filing her paperwork to incorporate, to take in all the stories in this book. Each mompreneur who has contributed to this book has exposed her authentic side, with no chaser. Many have shed a few tears while writing; that's the beauty of being able to allow your feelings to escape the deep, dark places where they are harbored.

Myself along with my fifteen contributors are very unique and come from different walks of life. We are everyday women who are mothers first and businesswomen second, and are aligned with the same vision of wanting to help moms who want to start or already have their own business. We have babies, toddlers, teenagers, as well as adult children and grandchildren. One of us is even a mom who has been battling the journey of Autism with her child. Collectively, we are mothers, stepmothers affectionately known as "bonus" moms, foster moms, and GLAMmothers. Last but not least, we are either fully self-employed, in the transition of becoming fully self-employed, or still working a nine-to-five while running our business. We know that even though true balance may not exist, we believe in harmony and understand that we may not be able to accomplish everything, but we practice how to be symphonic in everything we do.

The ups and downs, the highs and lows are inevitable. However, being mentally prepared for anything is what differentiates a winner from a loser. The sun may not always shine; there will be clouds and rainy days, but there is always comfort in knowing that what God promises us will be fulfilled and that He stands by His word. Having children, managing the family, and running a business is definitely not easy; I'll be the first to admit that. Still, it's possible to accomplish it.

I am excited to reveal to you sixteen successful secrets that you will only get from reading this book. These secrets are golden nuggets, and while many of them may be commonsense to some, most of them are not followed and are oftentimes neglected, which is why people, and not just mompreneurs, find they are not achieving success. So, put on your most comfy PJs, pour a glass of your favorite wine (mine is Lambrusco and Pink Moscato…LOL!), make a toast, and then drink to the secrets of success for mompreneurs everywhere. To many blessings and future success. Cheers!

*"I know of no single formula for success. But, over the years, I have observed that some attributes of leadership are universal and are often about finding ways of encouraging people to combine their efforts, their talents, their insights, their enthusiasm, and their inspiration to work together."*

~ Queen Elizabeth II

# A WIDOWED MOMPRENEUR'S PERSPECTIVE ON CONTINUING THE LEGACY

## Avonti Garrett

Six years ago, a part of my heart and soul was forever severed from my being. I can still feel the severity of my pain as I reflect on the day my husband, Stephen Garrett aka Static Major, my lover and best friend, was taken from me.

That night, Stephen was having trouble swallowing, and I urged him to go to the hospital. Fearful of hospitals after losing his only sister to a medical mishap, my husband wanted to wait a little longer before going for medical attention. Earlier that same day when he arrived at the Louisville airport from Atlanta, he was escorted to the car in a wheelchair. For over forty-eight hours, he'd been unable to swallow anything, and now his body was suffering from extreme fatigue, dehydration, and a drooping eye. Initially, I was shocked at his appearance because we thought all of his issues were caused from severe acid reflux.

Extremely weak, my husband lay in our bed and told me to watch over him. I watched as he struggled to swallow and constantly spit in a container next to the bed. Feeling helpless, I prayed and kept my eyes on him. Convinced it was time for him to go to the hospital, I finally convinced my husband to allow local doctors to exam him.

When we arrived at the hospital that evening, a plethora of tests were performed, and he was presumed to have myasthenia gravis, a rare neuromuscular disease. Doctors recommended he undergo plasmapheresis; a treatment that removes toxins from the blood using a central line – similar to a dialysis catheter. To receive the treatment, Stephen would stay in the hospital overnight to be monitored prior to his scheduled surgery the next morning. The nurse brought me a consent form to be signed and proceeded to explain the procedure they wanted to do on Stephen. One line on the consent form stated that in a rare incidence death could occur. When I questioned the nurse, she blew it off, saying the chances were unlikely and for me not to worry because everything would be fine. My spirit was unsettled, but I dismissed the feeling as anxiety and continued signing the necessary pages. When I finished, I looked into the eyes of my husband, who looked afraid. Again, he told me to watch over him, and I vowed everything would be okay.

Since his mother was with us at the hospital, Stephen asked me to run to the house and grab some of his things. Knowing he would be in the hospital a couple of days, he wanted his laptop so he could work and keep his mind off his current situation. Before I walked out of his hospital room, we held hands and he told me that he loved me.

"I love you, too, baby. I'll be right back," I replied, then kissed him and hurried home.

In the process of packing our stuff, my phone rang. His son was on the line telling me something was wrong with his father. Anxious to get back to my husband, I threw his laptop in the bag and hurried out the door. In an effort to remain calm, I prayed the whole way there. *God, watch over him. Keep him safe. Please let everything be okay.*

Minutes seemed like hours as I made the short drive back to the hospital in the pouring rain. When I pulled up, Stephen's stepfather was waiting to greet me and park the car. Still unsure of what was going wrong; I reached the floor my husband was on. Immediately, I became overwhelmed by what I saw…a chaplain staring straight at me. Nurses and doctors were frantically moving all about. My mother-in-law was pacing the floor and repeating, "I knew it. I knew it." That awakened me that something was severely wrong.

"My baby is still not breathing," she said. "They're trying to get him to respond."

They would not allow me to enter my husband's room, so I fell down on my knees right in the hallway outside his door. The family surrounded me in prayer. Out the corner of my eye, I saw a nurse grab my mother-in-law's hand and say, "Let's pray. Let's pray for your baby."

On my knees, with tears streaming down my face, I begged God to make everything okay. *Don't let my husband die.* Just then, two nurses, one on each side of me, picked me up by my arms and finally escorted me into my husband's room. A team of nurses and doctors were working feverishly to revive him. With every thrust of the nurse's hand to his chest, I could hear a loud breath escape Stephen's mouth. I begged for him to come back to me. I screamed for him not to leave me alone. I told him how much I loved him and that we needed him here with us.

"Baby, don't go. Baby, don't go," I pleaded, sobbing.

"We have to stop," I heard the doctor tell me.

"NO!" I screamed. "JUST FIVE MORE MINUTES. I KNOW HE'LL COME BACK TO ME."

"We've been at this for over an hour. I'm sorry, but there is nothing more we can do," the doctor replied.

An unbearable heaviness instantaneously fell on my chest, causing me to repeatedly gasp for air.

"NO! NO! NO!"

Before I knew it, I was screaming at the top of my lungs. I pulled down the curtains that surrounded my husband's body. I rushed closer to him, despite them trying their best to pull me away. With my eyes, I followed a trail of blood from his mouth to a bucket full of blood next to his bed. I reached over and lifted his eyelids; his lifeless eyes stared straight up toward the ceiling. It is then that I completely blacked out, and when I awoke, my mom was laying on top of me yelling for help. My husband, my children's father, was gone.

Following his death, I learned that my husband had complained to his mother and the nurses of intense pain once the catheter was placed. The doctor, who knew he'd made an error when placing the line, called the nurse and instructed her to remove it, believing it would be safe to replace it in the morning. As soon as the nurse removed the line from Stephen's neck, he lost consciousness. He never regained consciousness and died shortly after. An autopsy revealed my husband died from complications during a medical procedure - basically medical negligence.

For the next month, I couldn't eat, sleep, or breathe without replaying that night. I missed my husband and desperately wanted him back. One evening, I ran into my closet to throw a tantrum with God.

"I want him back! I want him back! How could you let this happen? How could you take him from me? How could you take him from us?"

Consumed with my tears, I ignored our daughter calling out to find me. Then I heard a knock at the door.

"Momma, are you okay?" she asked.

"No, baby, I'm not. Mommy is sad. I miss Daddy," I told her.

"I miss him, too," she whispered back.

"Do you ever cry?" I asked.

"No, because if I cry, I know it will make you cry. How do I pray, Mommy?" our daughter asked.

Intrigued, I lost sight of my pain and fully engaged with her for the first time in weeks. I'd forgotten she was hurting, too.

"Well, you just talk to him like you talk to me," I told her.

She touched my face and asked God to help me, to give me joy and to take the pain away. She told me it was time to get up and reached out her hand to me. I got up, and that day, God numbed my pain and slowly restored my soul.

Later that week while lying in bed alone, I felt a physical tugging in my spirit. It was as if something was being ripped out of me. I doubled over in pain, and as suddenly as it began, the pain left. I looked up in the right corner of the room and saw something move towards the ceiling. It was an image I couldn't make out, but whatever had been ripped out of my spirit was leaving for good. I've never had that feeling again.

My husband, Stephen Garrett aka Static Major, was a Grammy Award-winning songwriter, producer, and singer. He wrote and produced mega-hits for Ginuwine, Aaliyah, Destiny's Child, Jay-Z, Nas, Diddy, Dr. Dre, Christina Aguilera, Pretty Ricky, and Playa. Weeks prior to his death, he had just finished shooting a video for Lil Wayne's song "Lollipop", the number one hit he penned for him. Static was on set to release his solo album the year he died. It never happened; yet, his dreams, goals, and hard work over the last decade were not in vain. Static received a Grammy for "Lollipop" and continues to live through the music he left behind. Artists still purchase his collections of writings and produced beats he gifted us. He was most recently recognized for his contribution to the Grammy Award-winning Drake album as well as the latest album released by Rihanna.

The other day, I was listening to a song he wrote for his solo album called *All the Way to Heaven*. In one of the verses, he wrote, *If it don't rain, then the flowers won't grow*. I knew it was a message from him to me. The first three years after his death, I had a lot of rainy, cold, and dark days. During that time, our house burned down, the building I bought for the Stephen Garrett School of the Performing Arts caught fire, and one of our sons got into trouble with the law. There were days the pressure and stress drained all my strength and I couldn't get out of bed. I learned to be okay with that, but I also learned to lessen those days by talking with God more often. Over time, my faith grew and God answered my cries for help.

One night while I was praying for strength, God revealed a vision to me. It was so vivid that it seemed like it was already taking place. Kids of all ages were playing music, writing songs, laughing, smiling, and learning to engineer beats. Looking around, I saw a young man sharing his story with a woman, who was dressed in all white and standing beside him. He told her how the school had been pivotal in changing his once wayward life. He had been headed to the streets when he came to the school. Previously, he'd failed all but one of his classes, had no direction, and was the product of an at-risk childhood. As a last resort, his mother enrolled him in the school where he quickly gained a passion for music. After three years at the school, his grade had drastically improved, and he was headed to college; he would be the first one in his family to ever attend.

Flashing to the woman in white, I saw my own reflection. God shared with me that I would carry on my husband's legacy by inspiring his love and passion for music into the hearts of at-risk youth. I would do that through my foundation To Save a Life, which is the umbrella for the Stephen Garrett School of the Performing Arts. My husband was not just an award-winning hit maker; he was an adoring father to three children, a beloved son, a loyal friend, a hardworking entrepreneur, and my best friend. My life's assignment is to make sure his vision and legacy go beyond his time here on earth.

It's crazy how the biggest pain in your life can awaken the magnitude of the power within you. Myles Monroe said, *Joy in the midst of hell is the hallmark of those who have truly found God's purpose for their lives and have committed themselves to cooperating with it.* It took some healing and some time, but eventually, my mourning turned to joy. Even though I never got all the answers to the questions I screamed at God, oddly I got something better. I got peace. I learned to trust God fully. Through every twist and turn over the last six years, He has brought me through it all stronger and wiser.

When I was a little girl, I had a talk with God. Abandoned by my father as an infant, I was a girl desperate for a father's love. God told me that He loved me and that He would never leave me. He has kept His word. Even when I feel alone, He has intentionally shown me where He carried me. I don't worry much these days, but if I start to, God reminds me of His promises to love and stay with me. Every time I come to another roadblock in my life, God sends me someone to speak life into my situation and guide me on my journey. As I have entrusted myself completely to God's will for my life, He has taken everything the enemy meant for my destruction and turned it around for my good. In His love and grace towards me, He revealed my purpose.

Purpose transforms mistakes into miracles and disappointments into testimonies. I forgave the doctors and nurses for the deadly mistake made on February 25, 2008, and after that, I was freed to walk into alignment with the plans and purposes God has for my life. Once I let go of the pain, I started seeing myself as a warrior and no longer a victim. As long as I'm still here, I have a reason, a purpose, and a destiny. As a warrior, I fight for my children's peace. I fight to keep Stephen's legacy alive. I fight to help others. My greatest desire is to keep my word to my husband by watching over our children, the legacy he left, and to SAVE A LIFE.

Personal fulfillment is the only true measure of success. If you want to truly be a successful mompreneur, you have to know who you are, love who you are, and ACT on who you are. As you DO that, you will have more love to give others, especially your children. They will carry on your legacy, so it is important that they see your zeal for your life's mission. Our three children were ultimately blessed with Stephen's legacy of persistence, passion, perseverance, hard work, love, and a full life. They get to witness me continue that legacy. In return, they will inherit a blueprint and a launching pad that will take them farther than we went. They will have the opportunity to save thousands of lives; that's what our family legacy is all about. I know Stephen is proud of the work I am doing with our foundation, our children, and promoting his legacy. There are still days when I really miss him and wish he was here, but I know he is always watching out for me.

*"Success is liking yourself, liking what you do, and liking how you do it,"*

~ Maya Angelou

## Chapter 1

# ALIGN TO YOUR PURPOSE AND DESTINY TO BE FREE

### Patrice Tartt

Staring at walls so dark. Even if there was sunlight, I still would not be able to see my shadow. Drowning in a sea of unhappiness, emptiness, loneliness, and deceit would make anyone want to die. I would love nothing more than to dance to the tunes of bells and whistles as I try to cut through the red tape of politics, but as soon as I look up and see the glass ceiling above my head, I know it is next to impossible. It was then I came to the realization that there was no getting passed that without being a brown noser at some point in time.

This has been my life for the past ten years, and hearing the key turn in the lock as my eyes remained closed was music to my ears. The bars...oh the bars. No, not like the bars in a hot beat that your favorite producer just dropped, but rather the cold metal bars I had been confined within for so long that would soon release me. Finally, the day had come where I would no longer be fed lies in the shape of bread, and no longer would I have to drink water from the cup of deceit.

As soon as the key unlocked that magical gateway to my freedom, and with the chains around my feet, I said goodbye to the darkness while being led out of the four walls that cast out the sun's rays. While putting one chained foot in front of the other, the others looked at me as I looked back at them. Their expression was one of happiness at the fact that it wasn't them. I looked again at them humbly because God had chosen me to walk this hall of shame. They whispered and wondered what would happen to me next. After all, how would I survive once I was released? As a single woman with a child, I knew if God brought me to it, he would bring me through it, and as a child of His, I will always be a victor. Even in my worst mess, it was so that I would be able to share my message one day.

April 22, 2014, I experienced freedom from being incarcerated and was reunited with my son. My mind, body, and soul were now free from the bondage of nine to five. I was no longer caught up in the corporate matrix. It was then that I could spend more time with my son, who finally had his mommy back full time and not just in the evenings and on weekends. The next day following my unexpected release from my firm due to my layoff, I now had time to gain clarity and focus on how my journey first began and my purpose in life that would lead me to my destiny of being free. I took a moment to reflect back on the previous years; this was a way to boost my spirits. I came to the realization that I was on the right track after all and what seemed like something bad would turn out to be something good. We can't buy time, and this meant I had more time to work on finalizing all the last-minute production items for the book and movement for *Mommy Divas on the Move.*

In 2011 while standing outside of my father's house, I felt my eyes and face become engulfed with what felt like a water main break in the neighborhood, entrapping me right where I stood. I never imagined such a day happening to me ever in life. The tears could not be stopped. My entire face felt as though it had been submerged in a sink full of water, and I started breathing frantically as though unexpectedly being forced face first into a tub of water where I had to hold my breath to stay alive before being released to come up for air.

I was angry, hurt, sad, and plain ole pissed off. How could so-called family members do this to me? Most importantly, how could they do this to my dad? April 2011 was one of the worst times in my life, and finding out the day before my father's funeral that only approximately four hundred dollars was left in his bank accounts was simply unacceptable. As beneficiary of all his accounts and being named in his will, I was completely befuddled. The betrayal of loved ones is real, and as taboo as it is, it happens.

On that day, I decided I would become a publisher and an author. My inspiration to start my business happened when I unexpectedly lost my dad to a rare disease called amyloidosis and congestive heart failure. In addition to this, I had family drama that I was forced to deal with only three months after my son was born. Shortly after, Patrice Tartt Publishing, LLC was birthed, and *Wounds of Deception,* my debut novel, was published.

Sharing how a tragedy could be turned into triumph is something I felt I needed to share with the world. So in 2014, due to my new love for writing, I decided to start a program called Girls Write Too under my publishing company so I could teach young girls how to write and become authors, poets, and bloggers well before adulthood. This would ensure that they got a head start and were ahead of the writing curve. God did not bless me with this gift so I could keep it to myself. I strongly believe in the philosophy of "Each one teach one".

"I could get used to this," I said out loud, taking in the fresh morning air. I watched the eagles soar high above the birds and delighted in the bright sun gently touching my skin along with the soft breeze blowing through my curls. It was a dream come true. Yeah, I experienced periods of worry, but that would only last for a few minutes at a time. Then I would remember God's promise that He would never leave nor forsake me.

While in a slight daze of reminiscing on how my journey began, I heard a faint voice off in the background. "I want drink. I want oatmeal. Mommy, Mommy, MOMMY!"

It was my three-year-old son, who was probably wondering why I seemed to be out of it. I had allowed everything that transpired within the last couple of days of being laid off to swallow me up like a hungry bear in a forest who found its morning meal. Being a single mother of a toddler can be challenging at times, but I wouldn't trade my role in his life for anything in the world. My son has been my joy and inspiration to be better and do better, although I have moments where I miss my father; my son is the spitting image of him. Whenever I am down and need a boost, simply gazing into my son's big brown eyes makes me happy again.

Raising a toddler and being an entrepreneur is indeed a lot of work, hard work. The key to being successful at both is to learn the balance between self-care, family, and business. This is something that can be extremely challenging to most. I will admit it has been challenging for me, as well. The balancing act of time management is no easier or harder than if you are single, married, divorced, or widowed. Life is always going to happen no matter what, and it is something we must prepare ourselves for.

Time management was a challenge for me, but not focusing on a nine-to-five gave me more time to concentrate on what was most important to me. Life happened to me when I was laid off a second time and depression made an appearance. Yes, you will send yourself, along with everyone else, an invitation to your pity party, but God! God will always make a way when there seems to be no way. I viewed my unexpected layoff as time to gain clarity for what I really wanted out of life. I was able to spend more time with my son, which is priceless. No one could ever pay me enough money to abandon my primary duty of being a mother, single or not.

My layoff from corporate America also allowed me to spend time on my current business and starting a new business, Mommy Divas on the Move, LLC. What better time to start a new business? Prior to losing my position at a top IT firm in the Washington, D.C. metro area, along with running my publishing business and working full-time, I didn't have any work life balance. I was always tired, stressed out, and thought maybe it was my extremely active toddler who was keeping me busy. Once I was laid off, though, I knew exactly what it was. I knew it was the job I had recently left that made me everything but a happy camper.

Don't get me wrong; I was thankful and extremely blessed to have held a position in a Fortune 500 company. The IT field is a highly sought after career path, but being aligned with where God wanted me to be in life was a challenge. My passion, destiny, and reality were in serious combat!

The battle was too real; I was not awakened to what was actually going on because I was not "awake" to the blessings that were soon to come. My passion has always been to run my business full-time, but reality had me clocking into a nine-to-five every day and not living in my purpose. Being an on-purpose person made me realize that my layoff was a blessing in disguise.

My goal was to start a coaching program for women who were looking to transition from a nine-to-five as a full-time employee to being fully self-employed, but how in the world would I implement such a program if I weren't currently in transition myself? This is where being an on-purpose person, meaning I strategically envision ideas that will elevate me to the next level, came into play. My passion and destiny no longer had to battle with my reality because I was now fully self-employed and walking in my destiny. Sure, I would have that lingering worry in the back of my mind, wondering how I would pull everything off financially. However, I walk in faith and know if God removed me from a place that looked good but didn't feel good because I was stressed, then it was the right decision. After all, the best for my son and me was yet to come. The biggest joy of being a mompreneur is being your own boss and making all the rules; however, they still need to be followed. Being the one to call the shots makes mompreneurship that much better.

Everything gets better with prayer and time because God does what he says he will do, and His timing is perfect. Keeping this in mind made things a whole lot easier. I won't say it happened overnight, but it happened. The biggest challenge I faced was the balancing act of business, self-care, and most importantly, family...and having enough time to do it all. I have been able to overcome this because practice always makes perfect. No matter how much I might dislike doing something, the more I do it, the easier it gets for me.

Writing out a schedule and making sure I adhere to that schedule ensures that everything I need to accomplish each day gets done. Whether placing Post-it notes on my bathroom mirror the night before as reminders to plan my next-day's agenda or simply adding my agenda to my smartphone's calendar, I ensure that I personally hold myself accountable. Some days I fell off track merely because I might not have felt like doing it; other than that, applying and implementing a schedule are key. Implementation is vital to success. Saying what we can do, will do, or need to do is great, but without works, it means nothing. Incorporating enough self-care time is important, as well. All work and no play aren't good for anyone. It is equally important to make sure that we as mompreneurs are taken care of in the same way in which we take care of our children, because a happy mommy makes for a happy family.

In order for anyone to reach their dream goal, they must be an activator. In other words, they must make it happen. We must activate in order for the process of implementation to begin. God definitely knows the desires of our heart, but having faith that something will happen without putting in the work is pointless. In order for an idea to come to fruition, you must have a point of clarity and know exactly what you want out of life and your business. If there isn't a sound understanding of what you want or if you are experiencing indecisiveness, then this simply means you are not ready and need to go back to the drawing board.

We must also get out of our own way so we prevent the self-sabotaging act of thwarting our greatness and shutting down our success before it even begins. We're our biggest enemy because our self-doubt leads to the sabotage of our potential success. So much greatness inside each of us is waiting to be birthed; however, some of us are not ready to reap the blessings that our greatness will bring to fruition. If you ever wonder why your great idea is not flourishing or taking you to the next level in your business, whether it be a product or service, it could be because you are not ready for where God is about to take you. We are all one meeting, phone call, person, or "right place at the right time" away from being the next Oprah Winfrey. From time to time, we refuse to believe it because again, we are self-sabotaging ourselves through self-doubt. Sometimes we have more doubt than optimism that everything we want we can have. Once we allow ourselves to be free from that bondage of self-hate, we can then begin to live our lives with clarity; this is the moment we will awaken not only our minds but also our souls. Once we follow all of those steps and are ready to birth that "baby", it is then we will elevate to the next level that is our legacy. Who needs an empire when you can have a legacy to leave behind? I personally prefer the latter of the two, because when you leave a legacy, you automatically have an empire. It comes with the territory.

In life, everything is done by trial and error. As a child of God, I personally believe you must have faith, but you also must put in the work. Again, activation is key! Faith without works is dead. (James 2: 14-26) That being sad, it takes trial, faith, and error to gain success to anything in life, especially entrepreneurship. Without trial, how would we know if a new product or service works or will be in demand by customers? The answer to this is quite simple. We don't! It's important to understand that in order to know if we have struck gold with something, we must first try, which is accomplished through trial. Stay the course and continue when (notice I said *when* and not *if*) we run into adversity, which is inevitable. Being prepared for the unexpected is necessary; we can't allow the unexpected to throw us completely off course when it happens, because regardless, life goes on. The unexpected can be anything from a job loss to the death of a loved one. I have experienced both within the past few years, and I have provided examples of how I didn't let either get the best of me. Instead, I triumphed over tragedy both times.

One morning, I woke up to the sun creeping through the blinds and my leg feeling as if it was being poked with needles because my son's sleeping body was lying across it. (I guess he snuck in during the night.) As I slowly moved him to the other side of the bed, I a huge smile came across my face as if I was about to take a picture. The reason for my smile was because at that moment, I knew for sure that being laid off, my son sleeping in the space next to me, and being able to truly experience what it's like to live my purpose was nothing short of being in the first seat of a rollercoaster. The feeling was similar to the car of the coaster moving up the track until it reached the top just before the BIG drop, and then you start to anticipate the fall. When the car finally plunges south, my hands are lifted above my head and the rollercoaster camera captures all my emotions—my fear, (which allowed my purpose to Face Everything And Rise to the occasion,) my excitement, my faith, and my relief—in one photo. My rollercoaster ride of entrepreneurship is fun and scary at the same time, but I wouldn't give up this rush for anything in the world.

My successful secret is to understand that pain equals progress to one's destiny, so you must resist the urge to quit.

Most times, people do not succeed in life because they gave up before it ever happened. Following through is a vital part of success, and in order to obtain success you must never give up. When the light leading the way during your journey to success doesn't seem so bright anymore, just remember that the harder it is to get to your destination, the greater the blessing will be once you get there. A successful business does not happen by mishap; it happens as a result of hard work, determination, and persistence. Through all of your trial and tribulations in life, there is PURPOSE in your PAIN, which is PROGRESS to your DESTINY. Ask yourself this: do you want to be aligned with your purpose and destiny so you can be free? If you answered yes, then you must exercise your faith while undergoing trial and error. Just remember to never quit.

*"God can dream a bigger dream for you than you could ever dream for yourself. Success comes when you surrender to that dream – and let it lead you to the next best place."*

- Oprah Winfrey

## Chapter 2

# QUANTUM LEAP

### Zelda Corona

Fear. Worry. Overwhelmed. Uncertainty. These are some of the emotions that smothered me like a house filled with smoke when I decided to leave my job of almost twenty-five years to start my business. These feelings took me to an uncomfortable place that was not familiar. I was greeted at the door by justification; she immediately took the position of why it was not the right time to start my business. Mental photographs of my husband and children flashed before my eyes. I was then offered my favorite glass of wine by false security, which intoxicated me and reminded me that I had a great-paying job. So why on earth would I want to let that go? Finally, trepidation cooked up a great meal and force-fed me doubt, exhaustion, and procrastination. My head was spinning, but nonetheless, I had made myself at home.

I worked in the healthcare industry, thriving in what most people consider a "dream job" as an IT Project Manager, and believed I had arrived. I made great money leading my teams through challenging projects while loving every minute of it. Things started to shift in IT, and although I was still making a nice income, I no longer found myself excited about my day-to-day job. My role had changed, and now I needed to readjust to a more technical environment. As a leader, I could totally relate to the need for the changes within the business, but as a person who thrived on interactive relationships, I knew I was no longer a fit.

I compensated what was now missing on my job with my adjunct faculty role at a private university. I had been teaching healthcare management for about five years, focusing on interpersonal development. I love teaching and was having fun, but a new normal was taking over; I was no longer in control. The changes in IT transformed my instructor position from optional to a necessity. I began having the *need* to teach. Educating provided me with what I craved so I could survive a job that was literally assassinating my integrity.

*Either poop or get off the pot!* This old adage rang in my ears like a school bell, and I knew it was time for me to go to my next class. My children had always been a priority, and I took pride in having a strong marriage and the confidence to make things happen. As I thought this through, I never doubted *what* I could make happen. I just wasn't prepared for the *when* and *how*. I was given a prophecy of the date that I would transition out, but as much as I was excited, I was equally frightened. I experienced fear of losing all that I worked so hard to gain but was also terrified of who I would potentially disappoint if I failed.

When my son was fifteen years old, life had given me a revelation that I was not in charge. I remember jumping in the van and driving aimlessly, not sure where I was going but needing to go anyhow because my son had been missing for two days. No phone call, not one single word that would lead me to believe he was okay. I called everyone that I could think of, but no one admitted to knowing his whereabouts. I decided to drive by the house of one of his friend's, when I saw him walking with another teenage boy. I watched him go through an alley, preventing me from following him. I quickly circled the block, looking frantically down every street and between every house. The strong feeling of defeat engulfed my body and I started to cry. The pain from my son being so close yet not being able to reach him left me distraught, devastated, and discouraged.

I sat in the car with my head on the steering wheel. Trying to make sense of who he was and who he was trying to become had drained all of the energy I had left. I remember by the time he was two years old I had planned his life. All of my efforts went into making sure he followed *my* plans. But, the day he ran away was my wakeup call. I knew then if I were going to survive my breakdown, I would have to seek the only one who could fix my situation. I started to recall those emotions and began to equate them to my current struggles of wanting to open my own business. I revisited the dreams I had for my son and the plans I had made. However, I had grown to realize that I didn't control his course, although I continued to have intentions for his life. Now, at twenty-four, he has made me proud. I had to quickly come to grips with the fact that *he* must beat to his own drum and create *his* own way. Right then and there, I knew I had to abide by that same advice…*I* am one hundred percent responsible for taking the necessary steps and following *my* dreams. Only God is truly in control, but if He gave me the vision, it was my duty to be obedient and allow faith to lead my way.

Activator. Competitor. Communicator. Motivator. I started to go back to what I knew to be true – what I was good at. I had these strengths for a reason. It would actually be a sin-and-a-shame if I didn't utilize the gifts that I was blessed with. I am organically led by my determination, and I knew this time wouldn't be any different.

As a mother, I wanted to be a good example for my children. I taught them to have big dreams, but I also instilled that it takes action to bring dreams to fruition. Taking action comes natural to me, and this was also a skill I helped many of my students develop.

I began to look to my passions to determine the right business for me. I wanted to do something that made me happy and allowed me to live my life's purpose. I coach individuals, helping them to develop the skill of turning concepts into reality; I possess strong managerial skills, which allows me to excel with diverse relationships; I manage complex projects successfully; I have the ability to flex my communication style appropriately; and I had a proven record as a healthcare leader, where I worked with senior executives and managed clinicians and front-end staff effectively. My resume looked good! So, I started doing my research.

*"According to CNN.com, baby boomers are the largest generation of Americans born in US history. They make up about 78 million of the nation's population, which equals about 35% of the American adult population. This age group generates about 43.5 million family caregivers who care for someone 50 and over."*

With the light bulb flipped on, I continued searching.

*"eHow.com reported that an adult family home offers an alternative for adults who no longer can live alone, but do not want to live in a nursing home. This is a place where adults who are not related to the operator reside and receive care, treatment, or services that are above the level of room and board…"*

I jumped up from the kitchen table and ran upstairs to my mother's room. She moved in with us almost eight years ago. My mother wasn't a stereotypical mom; she never overstepped her boundaries in my marriage, and she definitely wasn't the type to gossip. After doing my research, I wanted to share the exciting news I had just read. Normally, I would have screamed my good news through the house so my mom and husband could both weigh-in. However, my husband was out of town working, and I was excited to share this news with my mother because I believed big money was in healthcare. More so, this was a business she always wanted to open, but never pursued. My mom was a nurse of forty years. She had retired from her nine-to-five, but she was doing consultant work for another adult family home. So, I knew this would be a perfect endeavor. I would be the director and my mom would be the assistant director; two dreams birthed with one egg.

It was a blessing to have a strong resource on my team like my mother. I ensured that we focused on the strengths each of us brought to the table. I created a concise business plan that outlined the necessary steps we needed to jump-start the business and bring it full circle. My mom, on the other hand, worked on the clinical requirements and made sure we would be compliant with state regulations. This is also the strategy I teach my students – look to your strengths. If you do not possess all the pieces to the puzzle, then team-up with someone who can help you fill in the gaps. You don't have to know all the answers; you just need to be resourceful enough to find the answers.

Utilizing my project management skills, I crossed my T's and dotted my I's, but when I had done all I could do, I had to wait for the State to approve my license and for my client contract to be accepted. One of my previous lessons learned as a project manager was that I could not influence all of the moves because I was not playing the game alone. Even with this realization, I started to feel stuck, and I hated the stagnation. I'm a person who needs to progress, or I'll literally start to feel like I'm alone in a rowboat in the middle of the ocean and have lost my paddle - just coasting with very little movement. I look all around me, and as far as I can see, there is no sign of land - no sign of rescue.

On top of financing my business, which wasn't even open yet, I was now responsible for helping my husband sustain our home. The gas, electric, water, monthly lease, telephone, and business insurance bills started to pile up. When it rains, it pours; our liquidating finances were already suffocating us, when my husband was unexpectedly admitted in the hospital for Diverticulitis. The intestinal infection converted into MRSA, and what we thought was going to be a quick recovery turned his inpatient stay to three extensive weeks of horror. This affected our budget tremendously since my husband had joined the entrepreneur club fifteen years prior to getting sick, which resulted in his membership being put on hold.

I began to feel like I was in a game of tug-of-war. One foot in the door trying to maintain my new business, one foot preventing the door from closing, attempting to sustain our home, and my heart aching while sitting in the recliner chair next to my husband's hospital bed as I prayed for him to get well. It was definitely not easy, but I knew in my soul that *this too shall pass*. Nonetheless, my life as I knew it was slipping away. I was at the hospital every night after work for weeks. We weren't able to take our annual vacation, and simple things like my weekly hair appointment transitioned to a bi-weekly slot. I stopped getting my nails done all together. As much as I didn't like these changes, this was my reality.

Prayer. Faith. Obedience. Favor. These four words carried me when I could no longer stand up straight. These words were my bookends: prayer on my left, faith at my back, obedience to my right, and favor guiding my path. I felt myself starting to fall a few times when I paid my mortgage late, when I couldn't pay my bills in full, or when I couldn't afford to go out to eat and enjoy a really good meal. I had to decide what was most important at the time. I started to realize a lot of people want to execute their visions, but most people are not willing to do whatever legal measures it takes to make these desires come true. I honestly can't say I was totally prepared, but I definitely knew the Almighty had spoken and His word was bond.

*How do I control the need to control?* With my face pressed against the carpet, I begged for wisdom. One thing I learned is if you ask, you definitely will receive, but don't be surprised if the answer is not what you expected to hear.

At least forty-five minutes had gone by, and I slowly started to come back to the land of the living when my meditation was interrupted by the beep of the alarm clock announcing the start of my day. Before I could rise from my knees, it became apparent that chains of self-absorption had restricted me. I was laboring in a bubble of "finding my way" so much that I overlooked the fact that the path had already been laid and the work had already been done. It was painful revealing behaviors that I needed to change, but it was the only way to start designing my new existence.

I had put so much work into preventing failure that I was bankrupting my ability to be proactive. I stepped outside of myself and took a long hard look at me. *What am I missing that I needed? What resources can I tap into?* It is very difficult for me to ask for help. I hate to appear weak and needy, and more so, I never want to look as if I don't have it all together.

I picked up the phone and started making calls. I asked questions, and as difficult as it was, I asked for assistance from those who already had a successful adult family home. This definitely got the ball rolling and clarified that my compulsion to take on the world was a supremacy that I needed to change, and I had to hold myself accountable. I had to answer for what I was doing to Zelda – for creating the increasing snowball effect as I took on more and more, while refusing to just ask, "Can you please help me?" This form of self-sabotage went unnoticed because I appeared to be okay, even to myself. However, now my resolution blueprint was in the making, and I demanded it to be tangible. I knew if I did not stop this damaging behavior, I would personally be responsible for the demise of a business that never even had a grand opening.

I needed to take advantage of resources that I was ignoring, and it was necessary I acknowledge that my business was a new endeavor. Truth be told, I still had a lot to learn. Being brutally honest with myself led me to value my risks, as they became my teaching tools. I began to master the understanding of how to revoke personal destruction, as I came to grips with the fact that my vision was under attack and the assailant was myself. After this realization, I started to promote my purpose by doing my homework. I studied my patterns of self-sabotage and began paying close attention to this makeshift shelter that I call my "comfort weakness". This was a tattered, one-room shack that barely covered me from the rain. I would go there to get away from fear, hesitation, and the resistance to ask for help. I never invited anyone into my space because frankly, I didn't want anyone to know it existed. I knew this pretend escape was not a refuge; it was definitely time for a new dwelling.

I started drawing up my new plans. I reached out to networking prospects, created a marketing one-sheet, and made a promise that I would be vulnerable under God because he was my architect. It was important that my new design enabled me to measure my successes and foresee my risks. My sketch would have to lay out my next steps and prepare me for my makeover. But, first, it was necessary that I shift my perception of surrender and give myself permission to exhale.

Because I feel the need to be consistently productive, I always say sleep is overrated. But, life has a way of making you put things into perspective. I am learning that it is okay to push hard, but it is equally important to breathe. When I was diagnosed with stage IV bone cancer several years ago, I never let it limit my vision for my future because I always knew there was an ultimate plan for my life. As a wife, mother, and cancer survivor, I can testify that I have encountered many struggles, but I have also experienced profound triumphs. I smile because I am engulfed with an overwhelming feeling of promise and hope, and I am excited to know that we all have the option of choice. I choose to consciously defy self-destruction; I have decided to challenge opposition; and I will be deliberate about letting go.

I remember the trip my husband and I took to the Grand Canyon. It was amazing. I never felt closer to God. The air was clean, and I felt like the clouds were within my reach. While standing on that great mountain, I agreed to walk out on the flank with my husband. I could feel my heart racing and my blood pressure elevating, but at that moment, the risk outweighed logic. Although it was only for a few seconds, the experience will remain with me for a lifetime. That afternoon when I stood on the edge, I had a few options. I could have chosen to jump. I could have designated to flee. However, that day, my decision was absolute: I preferred to be free.

My successful secret is to create measurable action steps that will allow you to achieve your goals. I birthed five concepts during my struggle to start my business that initiated my success. I defined what originated the start of my destructive behaviors by identifying my triggers. I designed a new reality by creating a new perspective for an old plan through reevaluation and becoming comfortable with starting over. I divided my resources and filled in the gaps by asking for help. I demanded accountability from myself and stayed true to my new approach. I developed a measurable transformation blueprint that allowed me to monitor my accomplishments and manage my threats. I call this model the 5 D's – define, design, divide, demand, and develop.

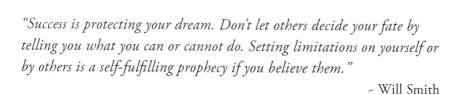

*"Success is protecting your dream. Don't let others decide your fate by telling you what you can or cannot do. Setting limitations on yourself or by others is a self-fulfilling prophecy if you believe them."*

~ Will Smith

*Chapter 3*

# LIVING A SUPERWOMAN LIFESTYLE WITH NO APOLOGIES

## Vicki Irvin

Nobody prepares you for motherhood and nobody tells you the absolute truth. Yes, babies are cute. Yes, they are cuddly, and yes, it is amazing to bring a life into the world. But, there is also a tough side to being a mother that is full of ever evolving surprises.

I was engaged to be married and having the absolute time of my life planning my wedding and trying on fabulous form-fitting wedding dresses. I worked out hard for my body and was excited to show it off when it came time for me to walk down the aisle on my big day.

As the thrilling day approached, I was caught off guard when I discovered I was pregnant. Surprised by this unplanned life growing inside me, I was admittedly unhappy. Truth be told, I never thought about having children. I enjoyed not being responsible for anyone else and looked forward to being a newlywed, taking fabulous trips, and living a party-filled lifestyle.

With my wedding just a few months away, I realized the form-fitting dress I planned to wear was not going to happen. Instead, I was forced into an empire-style dress, which was not my taste or what I desired. It was plain and drab, yet worked well at covering my growing baby bump.

Eventually, I got over the initial shock and became excited about the life I was carrying inside me. I went from being shallow, worrying about my dress, to actually thinking about motherhood. I was never the girl who dreamed about getting married and having a white-picket-fence house full of kids. I had been a young woman on the move, traveling with friends and enjoying being single. But, time was changing my heart.

I got married that July with a fast approaching due date in October. I rented out my house in Washington, DC and moved in with my new husband. I fell into the normal routine of commuting to work, attending my prenatal doctor's appointments, and being a new wife. While in my eighth month of pregnancy, I went for a routine sonogram. Up to this point, things had gone smoothly. Expecting the usual report, I gave way to anxiety when I noticed a confused look on the technician's face as she studied the image of my baby boy on the screen. When the technician left the room to get the doctor, I immediately knew something was wrong. The doctor explained to me that it appeared my unborn son had spina bifida, something I had heard of but never really considered it would be something I'd have to deal with. My doctor referred me to a specialist and sent me straight to the hospital. I will never forget the look of horror on my husband's face when I finally managed to tell him what was going on.

From there, everything was a blur. The specialist confirmed that my son had trisomy13, which is a rare genetic disorder that normally results in the baby not surviving. Instantly, I went from the joy of planning my baby's birth to the heart-wrenching wait for him to die in utero any day.

Following the detriment of this news, I was forced to go to the doctor every week to find out if my baby's heart had stopped beating. I wasn't waiting for life to begin; I was waiting for it to end.

After my third visit, I remember the doctor listening intently with his stethoscope. Then he looked up at me, and with compassion in his eyes, he said, "He's gone now. When would you like us to induce labor?"

Childbirth is painful, but being able to hold your baby in your arms afterward makes it well worth it. However, for me, having to endure excruciating labor pains and knowing all the while I would have nothing to show for it really crushed me.

I remember the nurse asking if I would want to see and hold my baby; I quickly said no. Why have that memory etched in my mind forever to haunt me? I was emphatic. I just wanted him whisked away immediately. Knowing my baby would have birth defects made that decision even easier for me to make. However, as with many things that are unpredictable, I changed my mind. After delivering my stillborn son, I wanted and needed to see him. Even though I held him for hours, it felt like only a few minutes. Before being discharged from the hospital, they provided me with a set of his footprints and the newborn hat they put on his head. That's all the memories I have of my firstborn son.

Having no desire to see or talk to anyone, I went home to heal and take the necessary time I required to get myself together. Astonishingly, my yearning to be left alone only lasted a few days. In my mind, I figured getting back to my normal routine would help me forget about things and move on. Anything to speed up the healing process, because the pain I felt was too much to bear. Against the advice of everyone, including my boss, I was back at work within a matter of days. I felt this was the absolute best thing for me and found myself feeling happy again. Consequently, shortly after returning to work, my temporary happiness turned to a desperate need to replace my son. My pain turned to an enormous emptiness and only another baby would satisfy the hole in my soul.

In hindsight, I wish someone had talked to me about my urgent emotional decision to fill my void. Had someone recognized my decision was based on emotion, I probably would have waited. But, no one said a word, and within a few months, I was pregnant again with my "replacement" baby.

On pins and needles throughout, my second pregnancy bent with anxiety miraculously went great. I delivered a healthy baby boy and life was perfect again. Or was it? During the six weeks I took off to take care of my son, I discovered just how much work babies are. My husband had a business to run and wasn't much help. We'd just moved into a huge new house, and I was having trouble keeping up with my own self-care. So, there was no way I was keeping a house clean. Caring for a newborn left no time for visits to the gym, but I wanted my body back. I would have settled for a few extra hours of sleep. While people love to give you advice on how to raise up a child, they neglect the conversations about sleep deprivation and the slippery slope of postpartum depression.

One day, the baby was finally napping, and I reluctantly took the opportunity to sweep the brand-new hardwood floors that were screaming for my attention. With the first whisk of the broom, I broke down in tears. I was in this big house alone, exhausted, and sobbing over nothing, I suppose. I was overwhelmed with the challenges that come with being a new mom. Looking back, I know I had a short stint of undiagnosed postpartum depression.

As cute as my baby was, he turned my world completely upside down. I couldn't wait to get back to work. Being in the house all day with a newborn was not my idea of fun. My father-in-law agreed to watch him while I returned to work, and I counted down until the day came. As pathetic as that sounds, I eventually found my rhythm, as all moms do. Everyone is different. Some women breeze through motherhood and make it look simple, while others struggle to get it right. I started out in the latter group.

After coming out from underwater, I began looking at life differently. I felt as if I was more open to things and like I was destined for so much more than the monotony of commuting to a job and working for someone else. With the world seeming like it was passing me by, I grew restless. Instinctively, I knew if I didn't find a bigger purpose, I would end up paralyzed by my current situation. I had married an entrepreneur and business owner; yet, we had very different perspectives about work. I once thought he was completely crazy for some of his ideas, but this new mental shift had me more receptive to them.

At his request, I attended one of his mastermind sessions, and he motivated me to open my mind to entrepreneurship. I got energized and wanted so badly to have my "own thing" where I could make an impact in the world.

After getting advice from one of my husband's mentors, I decided to try my hand at real estate investing. I suffered a few avoidable disasters and unavoidable failures, but in no time, I had a winning formula. The positive results I experienced enticed me to grow bigger in my business and share with others the blueprint to my level of success. In order to do that effectively, I needed (and truly wanted) to start my own real estate investing program.

Honestly, I was afraid to start my own business, but more terrified to leave the safety of my nine-to-five. I was raised believing my road to success was to go to college, get a degree, find a good job, and stay there until I retired. Then I could collect social security and travel the world. So, taking the leap to do something new and outside of my comfort zone was not an easy thing to do. Not to mention the lack of encouragement from friends and family who just didn't understand my newfound desires to leave a six-figure job and flounder on my own.

Losing my son was the most painful thing I'd ever had happen to me. The fact that I was able to push through the pain made me realize I really could do whatever I wanted to do in life. Fear prevents many people from moving forward, but it's only an emotion. I made a decision to embrace fear as an opportunity to push myself to higher heights. Without it, you don't grow.

With fear in one hand and my formula to success in the other, my real estate investing program grew beyond my wildest dreams. The marketing knowledge I spent countless hours learning was now paying off in a major way. I started speaking several times a month and sharing my knowledge. At the time, my son was still young and would sometimes be at the seminars with me. Starting a new business requires late nights and incredible focus.

I remember diving in full force, determined I would make this business work by any means necessary. During the journey, I had feelings of guilt. I remember working on the couch with my laptop. When I finally looked up, my son had been calling my name repeatedly and vying for my attention.

I will never forget the look of disappointment on his face. Mommy was working again and had little time for him.

In that moment, I decided I needed a better plan. As women, we want a great marriage, perfect kids, to pursue our passions, and to have time for ourselves. Of course, it is much easier said than done.

Painfully aware that I needed to balance my life better, I became more conscious of how I spent my time. I put boundaries in place for both myself and others. I was not willing to forego my dreams, but I had to figure out how I could make everyone who mattered to me happy. Guarding my time became critical. I trained people how to treat me and I was a pit bull when it came to my time. I discovered that in life, you make money, lose money, and make the money back again. But, none of us, no matter how hard we try, can ever get back time. Once it's gone, it's gone. For that reason, it is important to protect your time like the asset it is.

As I made protecting my time a priority, other women took notice. They began asking me how I was able to have a successful business and still maintain my family life. They wanted my tips on marketing and growing a business. They also kept referring to me as a "superwoman". With the increased demand of women looking to dive into entrepreneurship, I made the wise decision to switch my focus to helping them. I was very clear that the success of my first entrepreneurial endeavor was based on my sales and marketing knowledge, and I was convinced I could apply it to any business and get the same extraordinary result.

With the words given to me by so many women I encountered, I switched gears and created the Superwoman Lifestyle Movement, where I coach women entrepreneurs and business owners on how to grow a presence in the marketplace and attract clients for maximum business profit. The business aspect was easy for me. However, based on my own experiences, I realized other women were stuck or stalled because they were completely out of balance and overwhelmed. Yes, they had a strong desire to pursue their dreams, but the reality was that at the end of the day, they had nothing left to give. Maintaining a house, a relationship, raising children, self-care, and running a business are a lot on anyone's plate.

Remembering you don't have to give up one for the other and that you are equipped to do what you were put on earth to accomplish will help you through the most overwhelming days.

The dynamics of our lives are all very different; so, don't compare yourself to other women. A woman with no children can get more done than a mother with three children. It's a waste of time comparing yourself and trying to measure up.

When you make the decision to become an entrepreneur, you are making the decision to do more than most of the people in your immediate circle. People won't always understand your drive or motivation, nor is it important for them to. What is important is that once you make the decision to be extraordinary, you have to be ready to do things most other people will not. You have to understand and be willing to become a part of the 3% of people in life who think differently and don't always conform to society. You have to be okay with that and you have to develop a thick skin.

There will also be some sacrifices, but most of them will be for the better. Often times when women say they don't have enough time to work on their business, it is because they are wasting time in other places. Reality TV shows, entertaining other people's drama, and being the person to rescue everyone are things you have to give up in order to gain productive time back. Take inventory of the people in your immediate circle. Do they support and encourage you? Or do they drain you? Are they cheerleaders or dream killers? The decision to be extraordinary will cause you to lose a friend or two. Unhappy people have a hard time watching others move closer towards their goals. Expect it because it is coming, and although the lack of support may shock you and come from the people you least expect, it is definitely a part of being successful. Just ask any successful person you know, and they will have a similar story to tell of friends who have fallen by the wayside.

Recognizing my own struggles allowed me to empathize with women entrepreneurs and those aspiring to be an entrepreneur in the future. Our children are usually the most important people to us. My son gives me purpose and drive, and oddly enough, he teaches me something new every day. The common sense and innocence of children is something you can glean from. As adults, we tend to overthink things, and sometimes it's way simpler than what we make it out to be. The blueprint for my business, The Superwoman Lifestyle, was birthed out of the simplicity of what I call the *Three B System*. Business, Beauty, and Balance allows women to wade guilt-free through the complexity of motherhood and success as an entrepreneur by helping you keep it all in perspective. Your perspective, how you see yourself, will make all the difference in how you project yourself to others.

My successful secret is living a superwoman lifestyle through a focus on business, beauty, and balance. Your business is how you pay your bills. Therefore, you should never feel guilty giving it 110%. Being an entrepreneur is not easy, and the extra effort has to be there or else it won't work. Beauty is making the pledge to sometimes take care of you first instead of always putting yourself last. Exercise, eat right, and dress nice so you feel good inside and outside. A woman who doesn't feel good won't be able to give her business or her family all of herself. Maintaining a positive self-image is working from the inside out. Balance is making sure that at the end of the day, you gave the appropriate time and attention to the things and people in your life that matter most to you and that you go to bed at night feeling guilt-free.

*"Success is to be measured not so much by the position one has reached in life as by the obstacles which he has overcome."*

~ Booker T. Washington

## Chapter 4

# FINDING MY TRUTH

### Vikki Kennedy Johnson

Today, I simply beat to my own drum. I wasn't always comfortable doing so, but I am today. While growing up, I loved who I was but wasn't sure it was safe to let the world know. I worked hard to fit in with the crowd. I tried to see the world through a singular lens instead of the spectrum of colors and shapes that were vying for my attention. As I strived to be accepted, I started losing the essence of the beauty of my gifts. I lost my way while focusing on others who needed direction finding theirs. As children, we don't understand that being different is okay, because for the most part, we are "forced to fit in". We are often told to integrate our emotions, talents, and gifts into the dominant ideology of our communities. Many are more than willing to conform because they don't want the responsibility that comes with standing out in the crowd. They lose themselves and often never regain that child-like sense of being. Eventually, I discovered that blending in was suffocating who I was born to be.

My journey to authenticity was a privately complex one, although I made it look easy publicly. There were many moments when I felt like I did not belong. I often found myself trying to prove who I was to people who could not grasp the road God had paved just for me. It was very lonely at times. Yet, it presented wonderful and wonder-filled relationships along the way. Through my journey, I became familiar with isolation and learned valuable lessons. I also had the opportunity to experience the varied emotions of others in my circle because I was intimately acquainted with and intrigued by their issues, and often too excited to "fix them" while ignoring the roar of my own soul. In an attempt to prove my friendship and commitment, I now know I was too loyal at times. Frequently, I did not receive the same devotion. Eventually, I learned to prioritize from the inside out and now understand we don't always reap from the fields where we have sown. We simply have to trust that all things work for our good – even when they don't feel good.

I fought to be strong in my conviction to walk the road that God had provided. As an adolescent, I recall being a proud cookie-selling, badge-collecting, community-helping Girl Scout who was faithful in supporting the mission of Girl Scouts Incorporated. Spending time with other girls always felt magical to me, so I was always elated to hang out with my troop.

I remember one summer while at Girl Scouts camp, a group of us were at the lake putting our feet in the water and barely getting our swimsuits wet. At some point, a few of the girls started jumping in the lake to show off their swimming skills. Not wanting to feel left out, I sought to show off what I could do, too. So, I followed them as they swam across the lake. At first, I was walking on the bottom of the lake and moving my arms as if I was swimming. Then…the bottom disappeared! When I opened my eyes, I only saw murky, brown water surrounding me. That's when I remembered…*I couldn't swim*! Crazy…I know, but I did not want to stand out as the little black girl who could not swim. I was determined to be just like them. As I began to sink, I knew at that moment I was going to die. As my short life flashed before me, I felt my body being pulled out of the water. That day, the lifeguard (I still remember her red swimsuit) saved my life in more ways than one. I almost died because I wanted to follow the crowd. In that moment, I decided I would never follow the crowd again. I went on to become a trained swimmer, a lifeguard, and a water safety instructor.

As my talents became more pronounced, I became more confident. I started to embrace my strengths and take pride in my heritage. I am a descendent of a medicine man. I am a descendent of women who advocated for other women. I am a descendent of history makers who challenged the status quo and blazed trails for others to follow. As a child, my family spoke of my spiritual gifts and noted my intuitive abilities. I am extremely sensitive to the energy around me. I instinctively know when things are not aligned properly. I now love what I call "soulitude". My love for nature runs through my blood. I wake each morning with the excitement of Mother Nature peeking through my window with new opportunities to explore the beauty and complexity of our world. I am a child of the earth. I love to feel the ground beneath my feet. I enjoy the rays of the sun kissing my skin and listening to the music of birds. I realized I was always connected to the energy of humanity and just needed to walk in my purpose unapologetically. Truth be told, I could be a beach bum and be very happy. However, I knew God had much more in store for me.

The experiences I had as a child impacted my decisions as an adult. Children do learn what they live. My parents divorced when I was nine. It affected me more than I understood at the time. I was a daddy's girl, and he was the light of my life. He told me that I could do anything, and I believed him. I walked away from my parents' divorce believing if I went that extra mile for a man, he would not walk away from me. I took this thinking into every relationship I had for years to come. I carried the weight of each relationship hoping if I did everything right, it was a recipe for success. I became good at faking happiness and tolerating foolishness. I felt if I "showed" love (meaning looked the other way and didn't rock the boat), maybe I would start to feel just as loved. I never placed requirements on the men I dated because I did not want to relive the day that I sat silently watching my life as I knew it disintegrate. I carried that wound for years, and because I didn't heal it, I repeated it. I got a divorce when my daughter was the SAME age I was when my parents divorced. When I got married, I expected it to last forever. However, it didn't. The very thing I dreaded as a child I recreated ~ I believe ~ to heal my little nine-year-old girl self, who was running my life. Again, what you don't allow to heal you will repeat.

Over time, I made a decision to heal and was determined not to allow my failed marriage to destroy me or hinder me from loving again. With that spirit of living in truth, authenticity, and peace, I created a place for other women to live their best lives and move beyond their points of hurt. Supporting other women allowed me to stop focusing on my problems and concentrate on helping others.

I was and still am a free spirit in every sense of the word. I not only wanted to be a beach bum, but I also wanted to be a flight attendant. After college, I applied to every airline, but to no avail. God had other plans for me to see the world. I had no clue I would become a pastor or even write one book. So, you can imagine why I'm amazed daily that I have penned four books. While attending college on a full basketball scholarship, I changed my major three times because I knew I had to find some enjoyment in whatever I chose to do. Today, I can honestly say I love my life and all that it entails.

As a little girl, I always knew I wanted to have a big family. I envisioned raising seven kids, but once again, God had other plans. I never imagined I would give birth to only one beautiful baby girl. As a child, many strong and intelligent women who took pride in mothering, not only their own children but also the neighborhood children who may have needed some guidance, surrounded me. I was blessed to have two grandmothers who were very active in my life; they made motherhood look easy. My mother did, too; however, being a mother didn't come as easily for me.

I can honestly say I do not remember my daughter as an infant. I boldly admit that I "went through" five years of postpartum depression and came out of it. You can, too! Initially, I did not recognize the problem, but when I began having thoughts of doing harm to my baby, I knew something was wrong. During my darkest moments, my daughter was a reminder of my inadequacies and evidence that I was not a good mother. I knew deep down this was not true, but nonetheless, it was my reality at the time. I was in a deep hole and not sure how I was going to get out.

Like I mentioned before, I had great women in my life. My supervisor at the time and I had become great friends. Looking back, I now know she knew something was wrong. She and her husband often cared for my daughter when I couldn't like she was their very own granddaughter. They practically raised her until she was five years old. Now, as I reflect back, I know for a fact I only made it through because God and my ancestors were watching over me. I know they guided and protected me because I could feel their presence working in and around me during that time. This still rings true for me today. The ironic thing is if I had it to do all over again, I wouldn't change a thing.

The time I spent away from my child taught me how to plug into God. He was at the center of my life during this time, walking with me each step of the way. God put the pieces of my life back together His way. He allowed me to come out of postpartum depression stronger, wiser, and happier. I found joy in the midst of turmoil. I found strength in the midst of what may have appeared to be my weakest moments. I found love when it seemed to elude me. During this time, I discovered that being a mother is an awesome privilege and I had to go through those moments of crisis in order to be in a better position to help other women.

In 2005, I wrote my first book *Gems for the Journey* and subsequently released my second book *More Gems for the Journey* in 2006. The success of both books honestly took me by surprise, and when my publisher at the time offered me another deal, I released my third book *Addicted to Counterfeit Love* in 2007. Back then, my road to being a published author was paved by my daily radio feature called *"I'm Every Woman"*, which I did for seven years. The more I connected with my audience, the more I was able to hear stories of pain, joy, and overcoming. My daily commentaries resonated with women across social, economic, and racial demographics. I learned women have unique hurts that need to be addressed in an intimate, safe, and sacred space. So, I created a quarterly gathering called "Girl Talk with Elder Vikki Johnson" in 2000.

Determined to be true to the women who shared their stories and pain, I named my business Authentic Living Enterprises, which is the umbrella for my speaking engagements, books, Soul Wealth VIP Mentoring Program, and the newly redesigned "Girl Talk Unplugged, A Sacred SistHERhood". I released my fourth book, *Vikki-isms*, in 2013 and haven't looked back. I have found that when women are forced to think outside the box, they create some amazing results.

My ultimate drive for starting Authentic Living Enterprises came after my divorce. I knew I wanted to help other women "begin again". I knew if God could help me rebuild my life, He could do the same for other women, too. Eventually, I rested and trusted in my belief that God knew *what* I needed and *who* I needed in my life. My daily desire is to help women connect with their most authentic selves by giving what I knew I needed when I was in a rough place. I wanted to provide soul nourishment to feed their mind, body, and spirit. Making a difference was imperative for me. I wanted women to be engulfed with the energy I brought to the table—seeing none of me but all of God. Today, I am grateful to be a mirror for other mothers to see the beauty of their own reflection.

Four years ago, I gave my cousin a kidney. It saved his life and changed mine forever. I knew I was born to do it. Sharing this moment with my cousin taught me the beauty of enjoying every single second we are given on this earth. I squeeze every moment out of every day and take nothing for granted.

These days, I'm learning that in order to receive more, we must release what we are holding on to. God has not let me down yet. I've experienced divorce, foreclosure, abortion, bankruptcy, betrayal, and depression. When I gave up doing things my way, God showed me a better way. Sometimes we hold on to things that God is asking us to release. We hold them for a variety of reasons, and frequently, they are in the way of better. I personally held on to some things for too long because they were my comfort zone, even if it wasn't good for me. We must realize things do not define who we are or what we are to become. I realized I was more than a wife, more than a business, and more than my possessions. I am a woman first! I am a woman who wants to change the world through my passion.

My journey to this point has not been easy, but it has definitely been worth it. With each business venture, I never allowed fear to stop the possibilities of success. Somehow, I always found a way, and YOU CAN, TOO. This may seem odd, but trust me when I say you will find success in your failures. Each failure equips you with a new skillset that you will need for what's next. There is always a "next" as long as you are expecting more. Keep expecting more. If you cannot manage failure, then you cannot manage success. *Take a couple deep breaths right here*

All things worth having are worth working for, but you cannot give your all to the cause and lose yourself in the process. As you take bold steps towards your dreams, find YOUR center of peace. Find YOUR place of friendship and sistHERhood that is safe, sacred, and supportive.

I did not know my life would take the path it has taken thus far. If left up to me, I would've had the storybook life of a beautiful home, the perfect husband, and seven well-mannered children. That's funny to me in this moment. Instead, I have walked a path that has included lots of pain and years of uncertainty. I have not always made the best decisions, but I've tried to honor them as an example of survival to women and girls everywhere.

As you begin to develop your business and your business strategy, do not be afraid to ask for whatever it is you want, because a closed mouth doesn't get fed. Seek wise counsel from others. I once heard an older woman say, "You don't have to buy all of your lessons." This is gospel. If someone has done it before you, they have made mistakes. Learn from their mistakes. They can teach you what pitfalls to avoid in order to accelerate your growth process.

Create a strong support system. Create a strong support system. Create a strong support system. (No, your eyes are not playing tricks on you. I wrote it three times so it will stick out.) You will need one. Going into business for yourself, pursuing your professional goals, or being an amazing mother will not be easy, but it will ALWAYS be worth it. Your limits will be tested and you will need a place to go to recharge. I have made a vow to myself to always go to bed smarter than when I woke up. Invest in yourself by learning one new thing every day that will make you a better entrepreneur, a better woman, a better mom. I have learned to love me some me. Because of that, I can not only teach other women how to love themselves, but I can also model for my daughter the possibilities of who she gets to be in the world.

My successful secret is to create an authentic village to help support and encourage you as a mom first and then as an entrepreneur. We simply cannot be who we are and do what we do alone. I absolutely could not have raised my daughter without my family, friends, mentors, faith community, and others who were/are committed to our (mine and my daughter's) success. It is important to know that isolation is dangerous and pretending is a waste of time. When you need help ~ ASK FOR IT! I experienced postpartum depression and could not function as a mother when my daughter was an infant. My love for her and God's love for her through me gave me courage to expose my need for intervention. When you are on the brink of losing your mind, there is no room for ego. My breakdown was my breakthrough, and my village STILL exists.

*"One important key to success is self-confidence. An important key to self-confidence is preparation."*

— Arthur Ashe

.

## Chapter 5

# THE POWER OF DECISION: FAITH, FAMILY, AND FINANCES

### Dr. Monikah Ogando

I didn't so much "start" my own business, as I felt thrown into the entrepreneurial world from my corporate career. When I first started my business, I was recently separated from my then-husband, my son was five, my daughter was a three-year-old toddler, and I was in shock after being diagnosed with Stage IV Cervical Cancer. There is no Stage V. It was a stark contrast to my life now. I've since remarried to a wonderful man; my son is a junior in college; my daughter is graduating high school; and my business has garnered many awards, among them being ranked by Inc. 500 as one of the fastest growing companies in the United States. Every step of the way, I can see the next transformational step was never clear to me. It was unveiled AFTER I took the power of decision in my own hands.

My first job out of college was at a financial services firm, and I quickly found out Executive Assistant positions did not have much upward mobility. I deliberately asked one of the vice presidents, "Who makes the most money in this firm?"

She said, "The brokers."

To which I replied, "Well then, that's what I want to be. Will you sponsor me?"

She was impressed with my directness and clarity, and agreed. She also warned me, "You're going to have to study hard. These are not easy exams to pass," referring to the licensing exams I'd have to take in order to become a Certified Financial Planner and sell specific financial products, such as life insurance, stocks, bonds, and mutual funds.

I laughed as I got up to leave her office. "Is that all? I thought you were going to tell me something scary!"

The day the doctors gave me a diagnosis of Stage IV Cervical Cancer, my daughter had just turned three years old and I was doing quite well as a financial planner. I enrolled my daughter in an amazing school, moved into a swanky condo in Miami, drove a fancy BMW I proudly bought with cash. Yet, as I stared at the beach from my living room window, the words of the doctor still rang in my mind. *You have about a year to live.* The next few days were a daze. I had so much going on. The markets were at an all-time high, but our industry was in an upheaval. The Internet was fast becoming a platform to contend with, and our services were becoming so commoditized that others in my industry began competing on price rather than quality of service.

I had started working on a set of notes I compiled for myself as I went through these changes at work. When someone said yes to engaging in my services, what were they saying yes to? When they said no, what were they saying no to? How did I find the best prospects? Where were they? How did I engage them? Did speaking work better than hosting networking events? Did attending conferences that my clients attended result in a better return for my time and money than taking them out to lunch, golf, or some other outing? Something had to be working, because I was outperforming everybody in my office by a margin of 3-to-1. For every one million dollars, they procured in portfolio acquisitions, I got three million dollars, usually from ONE better and qualified client than a pool of them.

Secretly, I was seeing my doctor and exploring my options. Chemotherapy was a harsh option with little to no upside. Radiotherapy would be a last resort, but he was not giving me any hope.

"At this point, there is very little we can do for you," the doctor said.

I sent my daughter up north to spend some time with my parents who still lived in the Boston area, and while sitting in the dark alone, I had a moment where I heard my inner voice simply ask, "Well, which one is it? Are you going to decide to live? Or are you going to decide to die?" Those decisions have quite different action plans when moving forward. As you can guess, I decided to live.

I spent thirty days in prayer, méditation, and fasting—drinking only water and ingesting nothing else. Then I followed up with a raw food diet and changed all my personal care products to organic or natural—no chemicals and nothing artificial. The way to kill any kind of disease in the body is to fuel the body with oxygen, which is why exercise is vital even if just a twenty-minute daily walk, and starve the disease from acidic environment. The more balanced and well alkalized your body is, the better. I also wrote incessantly in my journal and kept a notepad wherever I went, because I knew I had to not only release the toxicity from my body, but from my thoughts, feelings, and memories, as well.

In the meantime, I was coming up on a performance review at work. The feedback was very poor. In fact, they were considering firing me. The one saving grace was the curriculum I developed to codify the way I attract, engage, contract, and retain clients in such turbulent market conditions. This curriculum quickly grew into a program I was teaching across the nation for them. They wanted to keep my intellectual property. However, they couldn't just fire me, as I had not assigned intellectual property rights to my employer. As some of you may know, when you're first hired, one of the many agreements you may have to sign is a waiver to your intellectual property, agreeing that it becomes the EMPLOYER's property as long as you developed it while on their payroll. Well, I had signed no such thing, and now the tables were turned in my favor.

What began as a firing squad quickly became a negotiation table. I walked away having transitioned my employer into a client by shifting the working agreement to a consulting retainer. They would pay the consulting retainer for having me teach their sales associates, licensing fees for using my materials, and royalties for any derivative copyrights. I walked away from that meeting not with a severance package, but with a six-figure check! What a way to begin a new business.

I remember going to the accounting office to give them the particulars of this arrangement. When the clerk asked me who to make the check out to, I quickly responded, "Ogando Associates," thinking that putting "Associates" next to my last name would make my new venture sound big and professional! I rushed home to get on the Internet and find the Secretary of State website. I needed to incorporate this company with the state, get an Employer Identification Number (EIN), and take my documentation to the bank so I could open my first official business checking account. After all, I needed a place to deposit that six-figure check I would pick up later that week! *BOOM!* Just like that — I was in business. A brand–new CEO.

The first few years of my business were heavy in training, development, and coaching. I healed from cancer and have been healthy ever since, fourteen years and counting! I was not only teaching my curriculum at my original financial brokerage firm, which was now a client, but their sales associates would often bring their entrepreneurial clients to the class. They then would ask me to come to their companies to train their staff or coach their executive/management team members. I often find it humorous when people spend years seeking coaching certifications, and not because they are unnecessary or not valid or useful. It is simply that, in my opinion, the most qualified certifying teacher is experience, and results can be generated by the experience you gain. My business coaching expertise was earned in the trenches, with in-business companies that had real issues: meeting payroll, shifting brand or marketing strategies in the middle of an economic downturn or market upheaval, expanding or contracting staff or locations, managing cash flow, closing a greater ratio of sales, etc.

In the meantime, I was sharing parental custody with my now-ex husband. It was a contentious relationship, always tense, always on the brink of a tit-for-tat argument, and bringing things to court or mediation because we could not seem to act like adults with each other, not even for the sake of our child. Looking back now, I realize the best thing I ever could have done for my daughter was release control and surrender to the situation. Not out of resignation or learned helplessness, mind you. But rather to show her that you can be nice and allow people space to be themselves, while still holding firm to your convictions and keeping your life moving.

I struggled with feelings of guilt all the time. Was I traveling too much for business to be available to my daughter? When we were in the park "playing", I also found myself texting and emailing. Playdates were a God-send because I found a bit of relief in being able to share her attention with other moms and their children. Nobody prepared me for the tugging at my heart that I would experience every time I had to say goodnight to my daughter over the phone because I was out of town traveling for business, or the way I would be tempted to compensate with gifts for not spending as much time with her as I thought I should.

Fast forward to 2008. My company grew quickly enough to be named by Inc. 500 as one of the fastest growing companies in the United States that year. This was during not only the worst financial year in our country, but it was also a personally devastating financial year for me, as well. The award for me, albeit an honor, felt fraudulent. Or rather, I felt fraudulent receiving it. What if people knew what they were awarding me for had disappeared with the economic downturn? What if I couldn't produce at the same level of financial performance? What if I was in the wrong business and the tide had already sailed the ship? Did I have what it took to start over again? (At least, it felt like starting over to me.) Did I even have the energy, the self-respect, and the stamina? How would I rebrand?

With the help of mentors and mastermind partners, I quickly had to coach myself out of that funk. The blessing in disguise is that I had long wanted to rebrand myself and the company to include knowledge products and group programs I could offer to the small business market as a whole, not just customized to particular corporate clients. And here we were in 2008 with that very opportunity!

I quickly went into action. I launched new products. I pitched myself as a speaker for small business conferences and was invited to speak at many of them. I wrote and published my book. I decided to pursue higher education, which resulted in me earning a Doctorate in Psychology and a Doctorate in Comparative Religions. I married the man of my dreams, with whom I share a home in Atlanta. Discovering that I do my best work in partnership, I started new ventures with business partners. Having partnered with David Bullock, (author of *Barack 2.0 - Social Media Lessons for Business* and known as the Profit Engineer) to co-found CEO Mastery, and later partnering with Dr. Rachel Talton (founder of Synergy Marketing Research) to co-found Flourish International, is the integration of science, data, and numbers driven exactitude of running a business objectively. The leadership development of human beings is what I am so passionate about, along with the human touch, the human connection, the reason why we do what we do to survive, thrive, and flourish in today's fast-paced market and economic environment.

The important lesson for me, and what I hope to pass on to you, is that the calling in my heart was to express my passions and creativity through my business WITHOUT having to sacrifice quality of life. I still only work four days a week. I still take off to travel whenever I want to because I have built my business virtually. Therefore, I can be anywhere in the world and still speak, write, teach, coach, create products, and consult with high-level clients. Seth Godin once said, "Instead of planning and looking forward to a vacation, how about you build a life you don't need to take a vacation from?" I live my life by that ever-present reminder. It makes for a happier wife, mother, sister, daughter, and business owner.

Powerful questions create shifts in direction. I am a big believer in scientifically experimenting with my life. My career was launched by objectively looking at what works, what doesn't work, and what is missing. I ask those three questions after every event I host, every class I teach, every program I deliver, every client engagement, and even something as minute as my blog posts or social media updates. This way, you won't get caught up in your own interpretations, hunches, feelings, or vibes about something, and be able to look at it objectively so you can take your best and make it better. Take your ordinary and build it up to extraordinary. And whatever does NOT work, chuck it! When you run your own business, you can make those decisions and not have to check with anyone.

You must ask yourself what purpose does it serve. One of the biggest lessons of my life was when I took a theater class in prep school and we had a homework assignment to dissect every line from one scene of one act of a play. It forced me to think that every character served a purpose for the storyline. The dialogue, props, character development, and plot helped move the story along. It is the same thing with your business. Every activity, networking event, conference, and yes-or-no response serves a purpose. The question you must ask yourself is, "Is this decision I'm making moving the business forward or taking it in another direction?"

You must honor your boundaries as you clarify them. Your yes's will be more powerful when they are aligned with your vision and purpose, and when they are carefully selected. If you say yes to everything, the people around you will not respect your no's — whether clients, vendors, peers, or personal relationship.

How you do anything is how you do everything. Be excellent even in the little things. I learned this early in my career. Shortcuts that sacrifice quality for the sake of speed are actually speed bumps along the road. Take your time. Overestimate how long it will take you to deliver on your word. That way, when you are early, you can take extra time to audit yourself and surprise your clients with a sooner delivery. And if you run into problems, at least you have that extra time to work out any snafus.

Nothing is as precious in business as your word. Keep your word. Honor your agreements. This doesn't mean you will always keep all your agreements. However, when you have a reputation for keeping your word, people are more willing to be forgiving when you have to renegotiate a promise.

You can do this. You can do anything you set your mind to. If I can heal from cancer, and use the fear and uncertainty of that time to fuel my business into Inc. 500 ranking as one of the fastest growing companies in this country, surely you can launch your venture! You do not have to suppress or run away from your fears. Use them! You do not have to pretend. Some things just downright make you angry. Use your anger. You are not above getting frustrated, like all of us. Use it. Frustration is simply energy that you haven't moved yet. Put it into action. You do not have to minimize your connection to God in order to appear more "business-like". Use your divinity. Use your power. Use your talents, abilities, gifts, and skills. I call them T.A.G.S. We have all been tagged a specific way by the Divine. It is our job to bring our TAGS out into the world.

My successful secret is to decide. Homicide means to kill another. Suicide means to kill oneself. But to DE-CIDE means to cut off all other options. Making a decision means you choose an orientation. All your actions, thoughts, plans, conversations, and inclinations are oriented around that decision. No opportunities for second-guessing, no back doors, no doubts and half starts. Just make the decision to begin, to keep going, to start again, to ask for help, to launch, to be visible. Whatever your decision is, sticking with it is a thousand times easier than beginning again every time you stop because of fear. I promise you will look back on the journey and be proud of yourself. Not just because of your accomplishments, but because of the woman you became in the process. Then we shall celebrate the legacy of raising our daughters to supersede the path we walked before them.

*"The foundation stones for a balanced success are honesty, character, integrity, faith, love, and loyalty."*

~ Zig Ziglar

.

## Chapter 6

# OVERCOMING FEAR AND TAKING
# CONTROL BY THE GRACE OF GOD

### Alea Anderson

God always told me that I would have a story to tell, that I would have some preaching to do. I never knew exactly what He meant by that until "it" happened. I never imagined my pain, triumphs, and struggles as a divorced mother would be out in the open for the world to read about. I never knew my story would mean enough to tell and that it might inspire and give hope to others. I have always been a painfully shy and reserved person. For a long time, I was embarrassed to talk about the things I had been through. I kept them locked away deep down inside where no one could find or see them. I did not want people to think I was weak, and I definitely did not want them to know my once perfect little world had been turned upside down. After all, it was my fault, wasn't it? I didn't mean to make him so angry. I knew I could be a better wife, a better cook, a better housekeeper, and a better mother. I needed to shape up! Right?

Plagued with thoughts of worthlessness and suicide, I stared at my husband with a look of unfamiliarity. How could a man who I had known since the age of fifteen hide so much of himself? How could I not know? How could I be so stupid? Who was he and where the heck did he hide my high school sweetheart, the love of my life?

"I'm going to kill you!" he yelled as I stared into his eyes.

I no longer recognized him. A pool of darkness had replaced the love that once danced in his pupils. His lifeless eyes reflected no soul. The weight of his body on my chest threatened to crush me. His grip on my neck grew tighter as he gradually choked the life out of me. I stopped fighting, as my attempts to break free were futile against his brute force. I had given up.

*Maybe I shouldn't have awakened him to help me with night feedings. Maybe I shouldn't have asked him to help me bathe her. Maybe I shouldn't have asked him to watch her while I showered and used the bathroom. Maybe I shouldn't have asked him to hold her while I cooked. After all, the answer is always no! I shouldn't have upset him like this.* These were my thoughts as I struggled to take what I knew would be my last breath.

After I left the first time, he promised he would never put his hands on me again. We had just found out I was pregnant. The very next day, I found myself flying across the room and crashing into a television. I can't remember what I had done that time to make him so upset with me. He said I knew how to press his buttons, so I knew his rage was my fault.

That night, I left and ran to my mother's house, fearing for my life and fearing I would lose my unborn child. The next day, he called begging for me to come back home. He said he was sorry, that he wanted his family back and that he would never put his hands on me again. Trusting his word and being under the *Battered Woman Syndrome Spell*, I obliged. Against my better judgment and my mother's warning, I went back. He kept his promise throughout the rest of my pregnancy. Everything was okay except for the occasional profanity he would use to call me everything but a child of God, but it was better than him hitting me.

Now here I was again, fighting for my life. I heard her whimper. I couldn't see her, but I knew she was there. I had placed her on the bed in an attempt to save her from her raging father. He must have heard her, too, because in that instant, I could breath. As he released my neck, the expression on his face was one of disbelief and confusion.

"I can't believe I just did that," he said.

Coughing and gasping for air, I knew she needed me. Ignoring the pain that shot through my body, I swiftly got up, ran over to the bed, and scooped her up in my arms. As I cradled her small body, I looked down at her once dainty, pure white socks and realized my crimson blood had stained them. At that point, I knew I had to get out. Allowing myself to endure abuse was one thing, but I refused to make my daughter go through the same. I had some demons I needed to battle, but she deserved a better life and I would give it to her, even if it meant facing some of my biggest fears.

Fear had always been my best friend. I often used it as an excuse to remain stagnant or to avoid making serious decisions. I was now faced with the fear of being a single mother. To top it off, I struggled with the guilt of not being able to spend more time with her. I didn't have the luxury of being a stay-at-home mom, but I knew I had to come up with a plan that would allow me to spend more time with her.

God planted the seed of entrepreneurship in my heart at an early age. I always knew I wanted to be my own boss, but having my daughter motivated me more than ever. God really began to push me in that direction. I always had a talent for painting and designing homes. Although I had gone to school for art and interior design, I wasn't putting my talent to use. When I would go to church, my pastor often spoke about entrepreneurship. He would say, "Step out on faith and let God do the rest!" I always felt like he was preaching directly to me. I began to get convicted in my spirit about wasting my talent.

I never signed up to be a single mother! That had always been a fear of mine. My story was not supposed to end this way! We were supposed to get married, have children, and live happily ever after. Well, my happily ever after never came. Instead, I was slapped with the reality of a divorce and having to move on alone. Before I got the gumption to follow my dreams, people would always tell me how good I was at what I did and that I should start my own business. I'd politely smile and reply, "Thank you," but in the back of my mind, I was thinking, *Yeah right! How am I supposed to mold another human life on my own, work full-time, and be my own boss?* Plus, I was always scared out of my mind! My best friend called

Fear constantly whispered in my ear. I was scared to fail, scared to mess up, and scared of making a fool of myself.

Despite being afraid, I moved forward, but overcoming fear was just half the battle. I still had to figure out how to juggle life and all the responsibilities that came with it. It was so difficult and I wanted to give up. I was tired; I felt worthless and stupid from all of the abuse I had endured. My world was in shambles, but I had to find a way to keep going. Afterall, I had a tiny, little life that was depending on me to be strong.

As the days went by, I threw myself into my daily routine. From the outside looking in, it appeared as if I was on top of things and not allowing all that I had been through to deter or slow me down. However, just underneath the surface, I was a mental wreck. I was clocking in to a nine-to-five as a teacher, working at running my growing business, and trying to ensure my daughter had all that she needed. I would often say it felt as if I had three jobs. My days and nights were filled with work. My daughter was only three months old at the time, so you can imagine what my daily life was like at home. Bathtime, storytime, prayer time, bedtime, night feedings, diaper changes, and then having to get up at the crack of dawn to prepare myself to do it all over again. Can you say stressed out? I was slowly but surely going insane! I was being pulled in a thousand different directions. My job wanted lesson plans, my daughter wanted bottles, and my clients wanted paintings. Yet, through the grace and strength of God, I willed myself to move forward.

Saved since the age of thirteen, I always honored and gave reverence to God, but it wasn't until I was ready to wave the white flag and give up on life that my relationship with Him was strengthened and catapulted to a higher level. I vividly remember the day I realized I needed God more than ever. I was at church with a heavy heart and at the end of my rope. So, I got up and laid it all on the altar. I told God, "Here, you take it, because this load is too heavy for me to bear."

God made it where I had to be TOTALLY dependent upon Him. He made me realize all my strength came from Him and that I could do absolutely nothing without Him, yet everything with Him. He allowed me to be broken by the load of life and all I had gone through, so I had no other choice than to put all of my trust in Him in order for me to be put back together by Him. He wanted to build a better, stronger me.

So, I let God take over every aspect of my life. I allowed Him to heal my heart and mind by seeking therapy and learning to forgive. I learned that the abuse I endured was not my fault and that leaving my marriage was the best thing I could have ever done for my daughter and me. I allowed Him to show me how to be a better, more patient, more organized mother, entrepreneur, and teacher who could handle the struggles of juggling it all. He taught me how to slap fear in the face and tell it to "get to stepping!"

I realized everything I had been through was for a reason. I now know there were "seasons" that God wanted me to go through. Each season was critical in my life to learn things only He could teach me. By learning to overcome the fear of becoming a single mother, I learned to take control of all the other fear in my life. Equipped with renewed strength, I put one foot in front of the other and began to fearlessly make plans for my future by doing what I knew it would take to thrive and survive. Before I knew it, I was making strides to reach my goal of balancing work, entrepreneurship, and being the best mother that I could be! I am currently the owner and operator of Allure Designs, a company that specializes in interior design and fine art.

My story is still in the making; I still have a long way to go. My ultimate goal is to one day be able to totally support my family with the fruit from Allure Designs. A long time ago, I was told my hands are my destiny. I know it will not be easy, but I also know that with God, I can do anything. And so can YOU! It is very difficult to run your business and take care of your household without a solid, organized business plan. An unorganized business leads to an unorganized, less fruitful financial and family life. Planning is key. As the famous Winston Churchill saying goes, "He who fails to plan, plans to fail."

My biggest piece of advice is to keep a business journal. When you have an idea, write it down! One of the things that helped me to solidify my plan was to write EVERYTHING down. Every idea I had, great or small, I wrote it down. I learned I had to do this the hard way. I would often have these wonderful ideas floating around in my head. However, after taking care of my daughter's daily needs and running around like a madwoman with my daily activities, when it came time to put things into motion, I had forgotten them!

Take your plan a step further by creating a vision board. This is an extremely useful visualization tool. It is simply a collage of things that you desire for your business. It could be a poster or foam board consisting of cutout pictures, inspirational quotes, drawings, logos, or slogans that pertain to your business. Look at your business journal and vision board daily. Put your vision board in a place where you spend a lot of time. I found it to be more effective for me in my bathroom. Some days I will meditate on my plans for hours on end. This helps your vision to become embedded in you. Once this happens, you will develop a true passion and your vision will begin to manifest into your life.

Another great thing to do is make "to do" lists. Once you write down all that needs to be done, you may feel overwhelmed, but once you start checking things off your list, it becomes very rewarding to see progress. "To do" lists are great tools for managing both business and home. They help keep you organized and on track with your day-to-day life. Set forth goals with realistic deadlines. If you're a divorced or single mom, you do not have the luxury of having the other parent in the household to help juggle the responsibility of caring for your child. If this is the case, you have to set realistic goals and deadlines for yourself. For instance, if you're the mother of a young child, the majority of your day is spent caring for them. There will not be much time available during the day to complete tasks pertaining to your business. Try to get things done during naptime, while they are away at school or daycare, or after putting them to bed.

Always set goals and deadlines based on your daily routine. If you don't, you will find yourself getting burned out and overwhelmed very easily. Do NOT beat yourself up or get deterred if you miss a deadline or don't reach a goal. As the old adage goes, "Shoot for the moon. Even if you miss, you'll land among the stars." This simply means, make goals for yourself, and even if you do not achieve them, you will pick up something good along the way. Running a successful business and home requires a well thought out, meticulously organized plan and process that takes time to master. You cannot snap your fingers and expect everything to instantly and magically fall into place. It takes time, patience, and perseverance. Everything is done in God's timing.

Having a successful business and family life may feel nearly impossible at times. It may even seem as if God is not moving on your behalf. Just know that He is always moving and has promised to give you the desires of your heart. However, it takes time for those desires to come to fruition. Many people do not have the fortitude to wait for God's due season, so they cave in and give up. But, Galatians 6:9 says, "…in due season we shall reap, if we faint not."

Always remember there are seasons. If you are operating in God's season, does that mean you will not have opposition? No. However, if you know God has given you the vision and called you to be an entrepreneur, and it is your season to move forward in that calling, God will give you the strength to knock any obstacles out of your path so you can continue marching toward victory! I often look to two scriptures from God's word that solidifies the Importance of timing and patience. Psalm 31 says, "… Be still before the Lord and wait patiently for him." Habakkuk 2:3 says, "For the vision is yet for an appointed time and it hastens to the end [fulfillment]; it will not deceive or disappointment. Though it tarry, wait for it, because it will surely come. It will not be delayed on its appointed day."

One very important thing I have learned throughout my journey is how to hear from God. Hearing God's voice and making moves according to His directions will result in you excelling in EVERY area of your life. Have you ever asked yourself, "Was that God speaking?" Sometimes it is difficult to decipher, but there are five questions to keep in mind when you are faced with this. 1) Does the vision require faith? 2) Do you need God's help to carry out the vision or task? 3) Does the vision require courage? 4) Do you have peace about the vision? 5) Does what you've heard line up with scripture? If you can answer yes to all of these questions, it is safe to say your vision is from God. If not, it is an assignment from the enemy. Proverbs 3:6 says, "In all ways acknowledge Him, and He shall direct your path."

My successful secret is to pray before you make a move. Life is like a serious "game" of chess. If you make a "move" or decision without proper thought, discernment, and the green light from God, the outcome can be disastrous and cause serious setbacks. I can think of several unpleasant situations I could have avoided if I had just consulted with God first. It is very important for you to be sure that every idea you entertain or every vision implanted in your mind is from God. Every time you are faced with a decision, whether business- or family-related, simply tell God that you acknowledge Him in that situation and ask Him exactly what you should do. If you do this, you can rest peacefully knowing that God is the master of your ship and He will never EVER steer you astray!

*"Ambition is the path to success; persistence is the vehicle you arrive in."*
~ Williams Eardley IV

## Chapter 7

# STOP THE EXCUSES AND UNVEIL YOUR WHY

### Ayisha Hayes-Taylor

Unlike Dorothy, I had no magic red slippers to whisk me home, but on this particular day, I did not want to go home. It was my last day at my full-time job, and I was scared to say goodbye. I had worked as an administrator in the same school for over twelve years. Starting fresh out of college, my co-workers had become extended family. They'd watched me grow, transform, and mature from a timid young lady to a confident woman.

When I started my career, I was a single mother of a special needs toddler. On this day as I neatly packed away the memories, I was leaving as a newlywed and mother of a baby girl. That once rambunctious toddler was now a teenager. I placed the last box in my car and closed the trunk. A river of tears left me unable to say goodbye in person, so a text message would have to do.

After all these years, my job identified who I was. I knew I was no longer shaping the direction of my future. My secure role at the school had taken charge of me. Pulling away from my parking spot, I questioned myself a thousand different ways. *Am I doing this at the right time? How will we make ends meet? Do I have any idea what's in store for my family and me?* Just as doubt tried to take a seat in my heart, a city bus passed by, and the advertisement on the side of it caught my eye. "Let The Dreams Begin" was written in bold, black letters. It was simple and to the point. I knew it was "my sign" and my answer to the questions in my head. Taking that step required much more than magic red slippers. One click of the heels was not enough. I had no more time to second guess. It was time to ignite my dreams…again.

Truth be told, I started my business six years ago out of my desire to compete. Having your own business was the "thing" in my new circle of friends. I researched for months what the business would actually be and finally decided on launching a personal concierge service, as its definition seemed to describe what I was currently doing for my loved ones and friends for free. I targeted my business services to women, particularly mothers, who were considered the small business elite.

Though I didn't realize it at the time, I had honed the perfect skills for this business while working on my friend's re-election campaign. When I volunteered to help her, we had just connected after speaking at a weekend retreat sharing similar stories and pain. She was a married mother of two and a local judge up for re-election. The personal assistant on her campaign had become ill, and she needed help. After explaining my lack of political campaign experience, I offered my talents to her. I'm extremely good at organizing; I thrive off to-do lists; I'm a people person; and I write down everything. Based on my willingness to help and her obvious desperation, she accepted my offer. I became her right-hand woman, traveling with her, keeping her calendar, and reminding her of appointments. Toward the middle of her campaign trail, she suddenly remembered she had forgotten the cake for her daughter's birthday party the next day. Overwhelmed by the guilt of her current mishap, she began unloading her frustrations to me.

"I'm just so tired. I have eight piles of laundry, haven't cooked a good meal in a long time, and now this! I wish I had someone to do all of these things for me."

*I could do that,* I thought. However, even though she was doing well, she couldn't afford a full-time assistant nor did she need one. Maybe a couple "mompreneurs" could share my services and me. I knew there had to be a name for this, so I did a Google search for "shared personal assistant". After just a few clicks, I landed on an article about a personal concierge service. *Yes, that's me!* You must be organized, work well with people, and be good at managing the details. *Check. Check. Check.* As mothers are making their way to the top and putting extra energy into their businesses, balancing their personal lives becomes overwhelming. Frustration sets in and guilt follows, leading to their dreams being put on hold. Many of them never awaken those sleeping dreams again. *Bingo!* I knew immediately what my business would be.

I used my friend as my first client. As a mother with a complete professional calendar, any extra personal time she had simply couldn't be consumed with cleaning or running errands. So, I gathered information on the price point of each service and came up with more efficient ideas to run my company. While preparing to help other women in my position, I realized I needed my own personal concierge.

I continued to work out the kinks while looking for more women to offer my services. The greatest reward was the repeated sense of satisfaction and accomplishment as I gave assistance to women going after their dreams. Lady Mogul Enterprise would provide balance to their personal lives as they poured into their professional dreams.

The idea of helping others was exciting, but the only way to make this business soar was to leave my full-time job. I had a few clients; however, balancing that with the demands of being a single mother of a special-needs child and putting in hours at my full-time job was more than I could carry. Just as I was contemplating a major move to increase my business, two of my clients halted their own businesses to focus on personal issues and my friend lost her re-election. With unemployed clients, my services were no longer needed.

Weary from investing so much into this business, I put my dream of being a successful entrepreneur on hold and turned my full attention to my son. Jamison was diagnosed with autism around the age of two. Up to the moment the doctor said the word, I did not know autism is a neurological disorder that affects the social interaction, language, and cognition of a child. The most daunting information she told me was that there was no cure. I left her office feeling hopeless, shaken, and suicidal. For the first time in my life, I was unsure of what to do next. All my life I've been a planner. I even had a plan for the plan. According to the doctor, the only outcome I could plan for was taking care of my child the rest of my life or putting him in an institution. Neither of those was an option for me.

I searched the Internet tirelessly and ran across multiple articles that claimed autism had a cure. I was skeptical and intrigued since the doctor had said with such certainty that there was none. I spent hours reading others' success stories. Many brilliant researchers and doctors have devoted their lives to recovering children on the autism spectrum. I would look at their successes, integrate their methods into our lifestyle, and believe in a miracle. I wanted change more than excuses, so I set out to fully recover my son.

I worked all day with children, but by the time I got home in the evening, I had no energy to work with my own. Our schedule was always the same: wake up, give medicine, warmup breakfast, help with self-care, put my son on the bus, drive to work, leave work, pick him up at six, cook dinner, eat, bath, and bed. Starting my own business during this time sparked my desires, but the flame dwindled as soon as I lost all my clients.

My son was about to enter middle school. Nervous about this transition for him, I again turned all my attention to his needs. His recovery was steady, and I was fueled by hope every time I witnessed a noticeable change. Fully engrossed with the demands of homework, cooking a special diet, financial burdens, managing therapy, and supervising after-school schedules, I had no time for my own dreams. After making the tough decision to shut down my website and stop paying for advertisement, I didn't speak of it anymore.

Almost two years had passed since I had a paying client, but I had too much chaos in my life to think about it. I kept "coaching" people to follow their dreams, and they always left our conversations inspired and excited to give their dreams another chance. Not only were they refreshed, but I was also because I was walking in my purpose.

Finding my voice again, I grabbed the exciting opportunity to host a radio show. Interviewing guests and preparing for the show was fun, even though it required me to devote a large chunk of my weekend after a long week of work. A very special guest who appeared on my show was my son! Though he struggled to speak clearly, he communicated with my listeners through his vivacious spirit and carefree laugh. Most importantly, he fanned the spark in me that keeps pursuing the fulfilled life he deserves.

Six months into my radio contract, I met my future husband. He was a constant encourager as he witnessed lives being touched, but mostly, he reminded me of how happy I was while doing what I loved. True to his mischievous sense of adventure, he proposed to me on-air during my birthday show.

Shortly after our engagement, I got pregnant. Oh the joy! Well, except for my morning sickness that was constant. I was beyond drained. How could I think about the clutter and housecleaning? There was no time for helping with homework; I was usually late for work and had no energy to continue my radio show. So, I ended my show abruptly in order to focus on my health and the baby growing inside me. We were married in a simple ceremony surrounded by friends and family, and welcomed our daughter into this world as a new family of four.

Like most moms, I spent every day of my eight-week maternity leave dreading going back to work. While I missed my co-workers, I did not miss having two full-time jobs. My husband needed my attention; he wanted to enjoy his new bride. My nursing infant daughter needed my undivided attention at least every three hours. With the whirlwind of changes in both of our lives, my teenage son needed me more than ever as he entered high school. All my energy was spent, and I had one week before my maternity leave was up. Quitting my job seemed financially impossible. We prayed together and chose more extras in the budget to delete. With careful saving and planning, surely we could make a way. Our budget said the time was never. My heart said the time was yesterday. Time itself whispered now!

Maternity leave came to an end, and I was jolted back to the limitations that bind up our dreams. I got up late and dragged myself into the bathroom, trying not to think about leaving my baby and the exhaustion of a demanding job that took all of me from sunup to sundown. The excitement of having a well-paid job and secure place to work was gone.

I stood in front of the mirror, and in the lower right corner, the reflection of my daughter cooing in the next room suddenly captured my attention. She was staring at me, studying intently every move I made. At that moment, I was teaching her about the meaning of life. I remembered my mother quoting the Biblical axiom, "Train up a child in the way they should go." What was I training my tiny daughter to be? I prayed my children would have a spirit of leadership and entrepreneurial gifts. Yet, that's not what I was teaching in that moment. Suddenly, I realized the way they would get there was for me to show them how!

When you find your WHY in life, you stop figuring out reasons not to pursue your dreams. If the WHY is real, it will fan the faintest sparks into a blaze. It is the passion you need as a mompreneur!

My approaching birthday meant dinner out. I wasn't thrilled about the extra thirty pounds that created a visible bulge in my favorite dress, but I took hold of my husband's hand as the hostess led us to our table. As I turned past an oddly placed partition, I heard "SURPRISE!" Forty of my closest friends and family were standing there waiting to celebrate! My husband had pulled off the entire event without the slightest suspicion on my part.

After the initial shock, I told him that he should go into business throwing surprise parties since he'd done such an amazing job. He laughed and replied, "I thought about that, but I don't like doing the paperwork. So, I would need you to be my assistant." There was no time to talk. The noise of our crying baby rose above the chatter of the birthday party. As I got up to feed her, my husband left for his second job.

Several weeks later, my husband called me at work. "What do you think about me opening a business?" he asked.

"I think it would be a great idea. What would your business be?"

He mentioned the one he was sure would fit him best. "A personal concierge service. Have you ever heard of that?" he questioned.

I'm sure you can figure out what I said next. From there, a vision was cast, and I got busy making things happen.

The old adage "To fail to plan is to plan to fail" applies to every new business. Knowing this, I immediately began constructing the steps I would take for permanent success. I made a list of resources and connections that would be necessary for a strong start. I determined how the business would have a competitive edge over other more established and larger services, then started a blog to communicate to potential clients what I would offer. Once I was able to explain my vision, I began contacting people to join me at a launch party. The lower the budget, the greater the innovation has to be! I asked friends to blast my business through Facebook and Twitter, and I used my radio contacts to market me as a guest on their shows. I contacted mentors and other business experts, asking them to write guest blogs about my business and the need it would fill. It's amazing how a vision is clarified when you share it with someone and they write it back to you!

I visualized how I would present to the crowd who attended my launch party, fully preparing myself to sign the contracts that would come about as a result. I invited 150 friends and small business owners to the launch, asking each of them to bring a friend, and I was delighted to serve 118 people. Each guest filled out a connection card that included their potential needs and what they would do to recommend the business to others. That evening, five clients booked my services, and I made ten additional appointments with potential clients.

Lady Mogul Enterprise was up and running again, but this time, stronger than ever! I now have a team that contributes creative ideas and a list of business liaisons that work with me. Most of all, I have made my enterprise the ONLY way, with no negative self-talk allowed. I think about the next generation, and the freedom to be creative and fulfilled while getting paid for it. I will demonstrate that the dream is real, and I will pass it on!

When you are ready to become an entrepreneur, it will be because you are driven by a dream and have a viable plan to achieve it. Most people never try because they are money driven. Entrepreneurs never work for money; they make money work for them. I had to find the WHY, and once I found it, I was willing to do what it took to bring it to fruition. Dorothy only clicked her heels to get home again, but a long road that gave the courage of a lion, the brain of a scarecrow, and the heart of a tin man preceded her action.

So, take joy in the process. I am successful today because I made the obstacles in my life a part of achieving my goal. As a mom with a special needs child, I have well-developed skills for managing multiple complex schedules at once. The heavy time pressures in my own life have given me compassion and understanding for the clients I serve. My radio show connected me to people who inspired me and refreshed my soul. My children make me want freedom and flexibility badly enough to work with an inexorable determination that gets results.

Don't be a loner. Surround yourself with successful people who are like-minded with a relentless passion for an achievable dream. Encourage yourself! The success of yes will give you more courage than the fear of no. Like nursing a newborn baby, I have kept my dream close to my heart, feeding it with all my strength and protecting it from unnecessary distraction.

Each day take thirty minutes to meditate on the dreams and visions you have, and be grateful for how far you have come. Through faith in God and faith in myself, I am moving closer to realizing all I have dreamed.

My successful secret is to find your "WHY" and it will conquer your "WON'T". Discover your "why", your motivation, and your reason for chasing down your dream of becoming a successful mother and entrepreneur. Once you are honest about your "why", it will help you conquer the fear of your "won't", your reason not to do it. When you have no budget, complicated schedules, and people calling you crazy for leaving your comfort zone, your "why" will keep you laser focused and keep you going strong. Let your "why" drive your thinking and planning. Once you have made a plan, take action. In all your actions, remember to take time each day to focus on your "why" in order to keep yourself centered and excited about the success waiting for you. Don't be discouraged if one plan fails. Re-align yourself with your "why", reboot the planning process, and let the dreams begin…again.

*"Put your heart, mind, and soul into even your smallest acts. This is the secret of success."*

~ Swami Sivananda

## Chapter 8

# LEARN HOW TO BOX SO YOU CAN WIN THE MATCH

### Joan Thompson Wilson

I believed in storybook endings and thought I would live a fairytale life… and I almost did. My second husband, my soulmate, proposed to me at church in front of the entire congregation. I thought he was coming to give his life to Christ, but when I asked, he said, "I have already given my life to Christ." Then he got down on one knee and broadcasted, "Will you marry me?" I was in shock, but that didn't prevent me from saying yes. Our wedding was not written like a typical story in a book, but because it was between God, him, and me, it was magical.

As a child, I imagined how life would be as an adult. My dreams for my future were filled with adventure, success, happiness, and all the wonderful things I could envision life would bring. My future family would live in a house surrounded by a white picket fence, with my children playing in the yard. Eventually, I would be watching my grandchildren playing in that same yard as I sat in the swing on my wrap-around porch with my husband of many years. I was convinced my career would be filled with continued successes and void of any struggles. Boy, was I wrong!

As a mother of two beautiful, grown boys, a grandmother, and the widow of an amazing man, I have experienced my share of the most heartwarming joys and some darkest hours. During my bleakest times, I recall feeling like I had been engulfed in a tornado and pieces of my life were swirling all around me as I attempted to hold on to anything that would help secure me during this storm.

*Struggle.* That word seemed to follow me everywhere I went. However, the struggles in my life have actually made my life richer, fuller, and more my own. For me, the decision to start my own business did not come as the result of a clearly directed path that I always knew I would follow. Instead, it was born from a major brain injury that I endured after falling. While recovering from this accident, the man who I wanted to grow old with was there for me; he was in my corner. This is how *Corner Woman* came about.

Throughout my life, I have faced all kinds of adversities and have learned from them the difference between standing up and moving forward or being knocked down. My hardships helped to lay the foundation for the road I would take to get to my future. My struggles and challenges were very personal in terms of relationships and health, but were also derived from my professional trials.

Having married young, I traveled, in my opinion, the road so many women do. I was new to marriage, but I questioned God because I knew he had a sense of humor, and my marriage had to be a joke. My marriage was unhealthy, and because this was a core relationship in my life, my life seemed to take an unhealthy turn. Every time I went home, I would experience a sinking sick feeling in my stomach. I was in a deep dark place, just moving mechanically through life. My self-esteem suffered, and it took me longer than I had hoped to gather the strength I needed to make a better choice for myself. That marriage ended in divorce, and although it was a difficult time during my life, I knew I would persevere and find a way to rise above the adversity and struggles.

During those years and the years to follow, I fought battles with my health, suffering from one illness or another. Migraines, kidney failure, asthma attacks, high blood pressure – you name it, I felt like I had it. These illnesses seemed to zap the energy and zest for life right out of me. Looking back, I can see a correlation between the emotional health of my relationships and my physical health, as well as how these issues impacted my professional growth. I was being passed over for one job promotion after another, and my frustration would compound each time. I knew somewhere inside of me I possessed the strength to stand firmly on my own. I just needed the tools to do it. So, my search began for a way to build my own road.

Ah, there is a God! I met my second husband, the one who gave me the real relationship I had been longing for all of those years. The nights of swinging on swings in the park, walking along the waterfront, pulling off the side of the road and whipping out a blanket, popping open the hatchback door and challenging one another to a game of Scrabble. (Yes, right on the shoulder of the highway.) There is also something healing about finding a partner who supports you in every way imaginable. I had finally found a relationship that could enrich me, and as my relationship with my husband grew, so did my personal strengths. These are the strengths I would need more than I could have imagined. I started to come alive, be more, do more, and want more for my sons and myself.

While finally in a healthy, strong relationship that helped to fill me with positive energy and the courage to begin working toward my professional goals, I had the proverbial rug pulled out from under me. I lost my husband. I watched him suffer through a cancer scare and then have a fatal accident that eventually took his life. I wanted to crumble, hide, and literally not breathe. I did not have anyone to lean on in terms of support. Yes, my family was there, but my sons were the ones who helped me through the most traumatic experience in my life.

Just when I thought my life was getting better and I was on track, I experienced an accident in my home, which left me with a severe brain injury. I went from being a widowed woman who was struggling with each breath I took and much less successful in my career, to a woman who now needed the emotional and physical support of her grown sons once again.

As I adjusted to life as a widow, my sons were in my corner. The reversal of roles that I experienced was oftentimes challenging for me. My boys were used to having their mother, their own strong foundation, on which to lean. Now I was the one doing the leaning, and these two young men, ages twenty-four and twenty-seven at the time, had to find it within themselves to be the support I needed. As much as I wanted to be independent, I knew I had to allow myself to accept the support they offered.

Not only was my health an obvious concern, but my professional goals were at stake, too. Before the accident, I had a stable career, although not moving forward with promotions and satisfaction at the rate I would have preferred. Now, I was facing the task of trying to become strong enough to just *keep* my $100K+ career. Without it, I felt I might have nothing left. I did not want to burden my sons with my healthcare, much less have to burden them with my financial needs, as well.

Through all of the challenges and struggles that threatened to remove the hope from my future, I still heard that nagging voice in the back of my head – the one that whispers, "You can do this. You *need* to do this. You have the power to do this. You just *need* to find a *way.*"

So, I envisioned myself as a fighter. My boxing ring was life, and I didn't have all the control over how it unfolded. What I did control, though, was how I would stand in that ring. I could put my hands in the air and surrender, or I could put on my gloves, arm myself with faith, and let my determination lead me through the next round.

Soon after recovering from my accident, it hit me that I had been searching all along for a path lit up with neon signs that would "show me the way", when I should have been looking for a way to forge my own path instead. I should have been getting ready to knock down hills and plow ahead rather than being a passenger in my own life.

Those struggles were my teacher. They were my inspiration. As an employee and a partner in a failing marriage, I finally had enough of feeling like I was at the mercy of someone else. I also did not want to be looked at as the "widow" victim or as an "accident" victim. Starting my own business gave me the power back that all of these other things had taken. Don't get me wrong. It's not easy; it is not always graceful; and it's hardly ever exactly how I imagined it might be. What it DOES take to start your own business, after loss, is a resolution to keep moving forward.

Motherhood prepared me for much of this. During my parenting years, I balanced motherhood - a full-time job of its own that brings the greatest joy and sometimes the greatest sorrow. I always considered myself to be an active parent, even though for some years while my sons were younger, they lived with my mother as I struggled with my health challenges. The reality is, however, that balancing motherhood, careers, and personal relationships is almost impossible without feeling as if at least one of those areas is being neglected. When I worked long hours, I worried that my children were not getting enough of my attention. When I spent time and energy on my family, I stressed that my career goals were suffering. This game of balance is not easy, and it's a vicious cycle.

Losing my second husband could have led me to a life where I soaked in the sadness and let grief steer my journey. However, I knew I couldn't let my survivor's guilt shape my life. I had to take those wonderful, supportive lessons from my husband and turn them into positive energies and memories for a future life without him.

One of the first things I did on my journey to starting my business after the loss of my husband was give myself permission to take time for motherhood. Even with grown children, there needs to be focused energy and strength. Instead of turning away from my children to pursue my goals, I gave myself permission to put energy into my goals and share my passions and interests with my children. We all gained from the experience. I decided to get messy by putting up a good fight, which rarely leaves you without a mess. I gave myself permission to let my life look a little messy while focusing on starting my business. I reached out for help by turning to my friends, professional acquaintances, and my church family for help with anything from practical help to just praying for my strength.

Yes, it would have been easy to stay in that pain, to cry on the inside, and sink into a deep cavern where I would be left without the strength to survive on my own. But, I knew my husband would never want that for me, and somewhere deep inside, I knew I didn't want that for myself or my sons.

Then I realized I couldn't rely on someone else to launch me to my galaxy. I needed to take steps to get my career where I wanted it to go. These are the same steps I share in my writings titled *Don't Count Me Out, I'm Just Getting Started* and *Confidence, That's What and Who I Am*. They are the same steps I took to build the road that would lead me closer to my goals each day.

I realized if I built my own path, I would be the one who gets to make the decisions that are important to me. I wouldn't be relying on someone else to promote me or tell me what I needed to do to improve. I was in charge of my own failures as well as successful moments. I made a choice to be successful. I pursued becoming my own boss, creating products that would become my assets for the rest of my life. These products then became my living, reusable methods to generate income. My info products gave me the option to create when I wanted to and taught me about the topics that interested me. I learned several valuable tools for building successful products, and I have spent years trying to share these methods with others who have been in the same types of ruts as myself in life.

For most people, life is built from a combination of struggles and successes as they move through their journeys. Five key things have helped me to move beyond my struggles to find my success as an entrepreneur, all without giving up on my dreams and goals as a mom and grandmother.

One, I started to put myself first. This does not mean I became a selfish person. It means my life is in my hands and it is up to me to shape the future. I paid attention to those areas of health - relationships, emotions, physical health, and all that combined together to give me strength.

Two, I created balance. There are many things that create balance - or lack of it - in my life. Balance is a constantly changing component, but one that needs attention. When I felt like my personal life was going well but I was struggling in my professional career, it caused some feeling of being out of balance. I started paying attention to all of these corners of life so this balance would keep me steady as I pursued my dreams. I learned to gain balance and perspective from supportive partners, hobbies, community service projects, and dear friends.

Three, I did whatever I needed to surround myself with things that made me feel whole. I put on my subliminal fighting gloves. I knew I needed to become my strongest advocate and not be afraid to fight for what I wanted and needed in life. If I put myself first and created balance, I knew it would be a lot easier to plow through the challenges of a good fight. Sometimes, especially for women, we are taught not to be fighters, but to instead let other people fight our battles. However, every time you stand up for what you want in life, you get a little bit stronger. Keep fighting. You have the power within you.

Four, I took risks. When I started creating my own products, marketing them online, and managing my own small business, it was a bit intimidating. I now do not listen to that voice. I always remember that what I'm doing will require risks, but as the saying goes, without risk there is no reward.

Five, I gathered my tools. I learned to collaborate and surround myself with positive people, which is my first tool. Then I looked for people who have already done what I wanted to do successfully. Here's what I know – success leaves clues.

It is time to start building. Through hard work, determination, and working through the struggles in life, you can lead yourself to the future you want to live. If I can move through an unhealthy marriage to find a true partner, and then learn to survive and thrive after his death, even amid a health crisis, I know I have the strength to do pretty much anything in life. This kind of strength is born from adversity and challenge. It is the kind that actually makes a person stronger than he or she ever thought possible. Do not let your challenges be your roadblocks. Let them become your motivation for building your future.

Pain and loss is one of the hardest realities of a life filled with joys and dreams. However, experiencing pain does not have to mean the end of things. It actually means having lived a life filled with wonders and joys. My faith is the undercurrent that guides me through my pain. Believing in a meaning more powerful than typical, everyday struggles gives me hope. It is from this hope that I decided to take my painful experiences and turn them into gifts for others. I wanted to be an inspiration for my sons, granddaughters, family, friends, and others.

However, as an adult, I quickly grew to understand this isn't always the reality in life. Many times we are faced with challenges and struggles that sometimes make our dreams seem impossible. It becomes all too easy to lose that childhood enthusiasm that made dreaming so enjoyable. Throughout my several years of challenges, many of which looked nothing like the dreams I had imagined for myself, I fortunately had enough strength to forge forward until I reached the road where I could find my dreams once again. Looking back, I realize my dreams were not just sitting there waiting for me. Each step I decided to take forward through pain, loss, and heartache helped me to build my own road. I know I can do and overcome anything, and be the strong Mommy Diva I always dreamed of being for myself and my sons, Rick and Tony!

My successful secret is recognizing and knowing you can spar with adversity and knock out fear while gaining more confidence to increase your bottom line. I believe everyone is in a fight; it's just not playing out in a boxing ring. Therefore, I maintain a dream champion's mindset. When I feel defeated, I say to myself, *"Don't Count Me Out, I'm Just Getting Started©,"* and mean it! When it's all said and done, I want to be the one who is left standing in the ring. In order to make that possible, I must think and train my mind like a champion boxer - keeping my eyes on the prize, fighting through the pain, and never getting backed into a corner. Work to be on a forward path. It's okay to reflect on the past, just don't live your life in it. Use your lessons as teaching tools that you not only utilize yourself, but that you also share with others, because one man's trash is another man's treasure.

*"Action is the foundational key to all success."*

~ Pablo Picasso

# Chapter 9

# THE INFLUENCEHER WAY

## Rhonda Wilkins

"Sheesh!" I sighed as I closed the trunk of my Nissan. With tears in my eyes, I hugged my sister and parents, and said goodbye to my city of Rural Rome, Georgia. It was the summer of '89, and at nineteen years of age, without hesitation, a second thought, or a moment of regret, I was moving to Atlanta, Georgia, best known as "Hotlanta". My hobbies included singing and modeling, and now working two jobs with an attempt to appreciate "my new normal", I was no stranger to hard work.

I found myself all alone in the big city. Atlanta didn't care that I was California-raised, the second born of four girls (all three years apart), and that my parents, who dated from the age of fourteen and fifteen, were still married. Atlanta gave no chills to the fact that I was a middle-class, Baptist Christian raised in the suburbs, and my daddy served this country for well over twenty years. Or how my sisters and I became overachievers with the leadership of our parents, as well as our grandmother's strong influence of service to the community that paved such an empowering way the older we became. My grandmother was my first introduction to an InfluenceHER. Atlanta couldn't care less of my cultural background or the foundation in which I was raised. I had to step up and step out with a rededication to reintroduce myself to the city.

Although you never know what cards life will deal you, my dad always taught me to be ready to play the game.

Six years later, I adjusted to the city life, married the man of my dreams, and instantly became a mom. (Salute to all stepmothers, "bonus" moms around the world.) My husband's daughter, who was seven years old at the time, came to live with us for the school year. Since meeting her at eleven months old, I have always fancied my bonus daughter. Stepparenting, in my humble opinion, had become most challenging for me, especially with it being my first introduction into parenting. Not equipped with a handbook, sacrifices were made, promises were broken, doubt lived close by, and fear had a new home. I found myself questioning my parenting skills measured by this young girl who desperately didn't understand why her mom and dad were not together. The older she became, I introduced her to my vulnerability, my barriers, my unconditional love, my fears, my role, and my discouragement. Upon such an introduction, we both developed a newfound respect for each other. Ergo, InfluenceHER number two.

Upon this transition, no one could have prepared me for what was to come. For the first time since I began working at age fifteen, the Fortune 500 company I worked so hard for left thousands of employees without work. I found myself unemployed; this was such a blow to my ego that it created space for depression to creep in. In lieu of me confronting reality, reality decided to confront me. I sat face to face with what Mother Nature had given me and what Father Time had taken away. I had now crossed over into full-figure modeling, and singing gigs were few and far between. I had to face the harsh reality that my hobbies had now become my livelihood. As I continued modeling, it didn't quite feel the same. In such an industry, "fair" had become LEGENDARY, and I had just about had enough. I called a family meeting with my husband so I could share my fears, ideas, thoughts, and secrets.

With my background being production and management, I set out on a mission to show the world that full-figured modeling was the next big thing. For Christ's sake, this was a billion-dollar industry. I studied the industry, attended conferences, joined full-figured groups, and made connections to key people in the industry. I wanted to prove we should have equal rights and be thought of in the planning of the production, not an afterthought. Many times, designers would not even have clothes for us to model in. So, we were told to wear all black. Makeup artists always skipped over us because the slim models would be first in the lineup. So, they would need to sit in the chair first, oftentimes leaving no time for the makeup artists to do our faces. The craziest part is that with every show, the full-figured models would garner the biggest applause.

Maintaining my composure, I took every lemon they threw at me and made lemonade. I learned how to do my own makeup and hair. Every chance I got backstage, I would ask one of the slim models to walk with me, which help perfect my craft. I would volunteer to help set up or be on the planning committee so I could witness how the overall project worked. I was determined more than ever to change the perception of the full-figured model, and I was confident I could make a difference, especially with my husband's support. He better understood the struggles of a full-figured model and my desire to turn my hobby into a business.

It's one thing for society to judge, but when the industry was not created to assist in proper attire, placement in a show, credibility, and ridicule, I knew I had to become our advocate and solidify this industry. Therefore, six months later, I gave birth to my first project, Divas Unlimited Inc., an entertainment consulting firm.

After many saved unemployment checks and months of planning, it was time to produce my first show, paying homage to full-figured women. "The Big & Tall Designer Showcase" would sink or swim. Twenty minutes until showtime, I was a nervous wreck; before long, the final curtain was closing. It was clear the training we provided to our models, the designers we selected, the glam team that took great care of our ladies, and the overall ambiance of this event was well planned and none other than superb. The standing ovation brought tears to my eyes. That's right, little ole me received a standing ovation. The models, designers, sponsors, glam teams, event staff, and patrons all showed their gratitude in numbers with cards, flowers, and gifts. My heart was filled with joy. I stood tall, proud, humbled, and accomplished. It was bittersweet; the venue was packed, 800 persons packed. However, not every 800 tickets were sold. A lot of tickets were given away for an opportunity for me to embrace my community and provide them with a "Divas Unlimited" experience. I had become an InfluenceHER.

Due to The Big & Tall Designer Showcase, I was now the proud owner of a cultivated brand. I had become an intricate part of Who's Who in Atlanta. From this showcase, many jobs soon came, and boy, was I busier than ever! Not knowing exactly what we would be when we started, I simply wanted to produce events in the entertainment industry that were certifiably phenomenal.

It was a warm spring day when my phone rang, and I couldn't believe what I had just been asked. A representative from a nonprofit organization sought me out after seeing The Big & Tall Designer Showcase and inquired if we could meet about an upcoming project she had. Overwhelmed with joy, her request was honored. From this meeting, Divas Unlimited Inc. received its very first job. I was the proud producer of the Lupus Foundation, Atlanta Chapter Annual Fundraiser. Wanting to try something new, they requested us to produce a fashion show for them. Our job details were different from the norm. In my personal events, I was use to doing everything, but with this event, I was only to market to a select group and bring in sponsorship. Our bonus? If we sold tickets, we would get a percentage of the overall sales. Now I found myself embarking in new territory, marketing. It was amazing to do my first case study. The show was a huge success, and we raised thousands of dollars for an amazing cause. All had fun, and this solidified Divas Unlimited Inc. as a true production company producing for other companies.

With the success of branding Divas Unlimited Inc. as a well received production company, all I ever knew was to service my community and thank God for my project management training that kept me well organized. However, I made many mistakes along the way. I operated from a place of emotion verses that of business. I gave a huge part of myself to persons unqualified to receive and appreciate my gifts. Still unfulfilled, I expressed my sadness with my husband and knew by the end of my tearjerker that a change needed to come. Little did I know change was surely in pursuit; we soon learned we were three months pregnant. I was ecstatic and delighted that God trusted me enough to carry my legacy. Life was moving fast!

After the birth of my son, what a blessing it was to find my way back in corporate America as an Assistant Manager. However, the hours were crazy, and I still had to fulfill the obligations of my well-established production company, Divas Unlimited Inc.

The company had grown tremendously, but the jobs were not consistent, and with all the expenses that come with having a newborn, I needed to have consistent work. Divas Unlimited Inc. is now producing plays, movies, and productions for nonprofit organizations as well as picking up marketing jobs for smaller companies. It hit me like a ton of bricks; I could no longer wear all the hats. It was time to face the music. I needed help with my business. I was scared to let go of what I had built, and I was forced to outsource many jobs. I was exhausted trying to be a mommy, a wife, a manager, and CEO at my own business. My mind needed a mental break.

My son Paris was growing just as fast as my business. Frustrations within my household silently crept in. Back to work with high demands and my husband working with higher demands. Who had time to cook dinner? Babysitters became far and few. So, I found myself traveling back and forth to my hometown weekly to have my parents keep our son. I always believed in the power of the three P's: the first stage is PITIFUL, the second stage is POPULAR, and the third stage is POWERFUL. I had become stagnant in stage two, my popular phase for quite some time. People knew me and my name was floating, and people who didn't know me wanted to know me. Cognitively, I had construed this as successful.

Outside looking in, God and I made it look easy. Truth is, I lost myself in the process. Although feeling empowered, my "brand" had become my "kryptonite" both in the literal and physical sense. Funds were low, unqualified persons were in position, and I was experiencing a burnout. My son grew up asking, ad nauseam, "What event are you having tonight?" Communication between my husband and I had become minimized to strictly business, and my home did not have any equilibrium. With great liberties and what society would deem as a good life, mine had become funereal. What happened next surprised even me.

I placed myself in timeout, as I had often times before, but this time was different. In my expedition for peace and tranquility, I had to quiet the noise around me. My epiphany came once I understood that as long as I was saying YES to my businesses, I was saying NO to God and my family. So, I began to properly prioritize.

The first thing I embraced was the "sting", because once I was able to disconnect from the problem, it allowed me to connect to the possibilities of how it could be. Next, I focused on my team. I stared honesty in the face and redeveloped an "All-Star Team". I made a note of persons I wanted in position and then prayed about it. My winning team is made up of persons who are doing well in their personal lives. Prior to, I had persons in position for the sake of making them faithful. Being honest with myself,

I changed my perspective of self. I had to make my life more than just about me. I embraced my opinions, understanding that they had become my passion and NOT God's perspective. The enemy had used my opinions to disconnect me from God. Therefore, I discovered a newfound respect for my husband, the provider of my family. He does it all—working full-time, cooking, cleaning, and from school to play dates to extracurricular (karate, basketball, and football) activities with Paris. He was always there caring for our son where I once had been most present.

I plugged in and placed forth effort in providing what I call my recipe/embellishment of a healthy relationship: "FAS" (FREEDOM, ATTENTION, & SAFETY!) I revisited our friendship and began dating my husband all over again. He complements me nicely. As we all know, parenting can be most tumultuous. However, in my quest for harmony with my work and my parenting, I finally got it. It hit me like a ton of bricks. I realized that in order for me to move mountains in my parenting,

I first had to learn how to respect the rocks. Now, my son receives EVERY good thing I have to offer. Having given untold sacrifices of my soul, heart, and honor, blessed am I to hear that lil' boy call me mom.

In my professional and home life, I have had to overcome several challenges. Living in my situation, I always knew in my heart there were lessons that needed to be learned. I consistently prayed for guidance.

I can attest that starting your own business can be a bit of a challenge. Initially when I started, I held every position you can imagine. I wore so many hats that I didn't know if I was coming or going. Having minimal funds forced me to be resourceful. Many nights I was at the library, buying a self-help book, or browsing the Internet. I became the graphic artist, the web developer, the accountant, the sales rep, the marketing rep, the assistant, and last but not least, a believable CEO.

Being a successful project manager in corporate America had its perks. I had the opportunity to receive extensive training in diversity, marketing, sales, and customer service. Implementing and practicing some of these tools helped me to organize my priorities in business.

I will never forget the changing point of my life. I remember it was time for my evaluation, and as I walked in the room and sat down, I was instantly inspired. My boss was only thirty-two-years-old (four years older than me at the time). She ran eight departments, with my department being one of her direct reports. This young lady was sharp, smart, savvy, and demanded attention when she walked in a room. Her power was so exuberant, just like an InfluenceHER.

My boss conducted my yearly evaluation; I got a satisfactory score. She poured so much into my spirit that day. She encouraged me and recommended me for a higher position in the organization. She left me with the feeling of being empowered because she recognized my gift and showed appreciation for my hard work. Upon our departure, she handed me a book on teamwork written by John C. Maxwell, the book was titled *17 Indisputable Laws of Teamwork*. Practicing many principals from this book in life and in business is what led to several of my accomplishments in my seventeen-year journey. I have been blessed to work on some amazing projects with some of the best in the industry, but being honest with myself, I have to also give credit to my phenomenal strategic partners.

Some rituals I perform when empowering my tranquility that may help you as well are praying for peace and acceptance in both your professional and personal life. Building a strong team along with trusting and holding them accountable. Remember to never operate from emotion and always sow seeds that will benefit others. Become the InfluenceHER you didn't have, and envisage precisely what people expect to see. At every cost, avoid people's perception. Be sure to manage your emotions, time, priorities, and energy. Always pour out so you don't carry around mental weight, and don't celebrate history if you don't plan to make it. Never forget that every moment is a teaching moment. Therefore, sit under the tutelage that creates growth.

My successful secret is to embrace the InfluenceHER that resides within. An InfluenceHER has the ability to ignite social change and understands that their influence is not with all people. An InfluenceHER creates purpose in life and never asks for a hand until they first touch a heart. An InfluenceHER learns how to maximize their leadership with people above them because the higher your influence goes, the higher your impact will be. An InfluenceHER demonstrates outstanding leadership and is dedicated to helping the next person grow to their maximum potential. She knows how to break unhealthy soul ties by learning to say "NO" with no apologies. An InfluenceHER will shift from a life of ambition to a life of meaning. Her motto is sometimes you win and sometimes you learn. You are an InfluenceHER, and from one to another, create a platform so others desire your mantle.

*"Success isn't about how much money you make. It's about the difference you make in people's lives."*

~ Michelle Obama

.

## Chapter 10

# PAIN TO POWER: THE JOURNEY FROM FEAR TO FAITH

### Denise J. Hart

The day I got my results was a perfectly normal day. It was my birthday month and the sun was shining. Running late, I dropped off my son at school and hustled to get to my doctor's appointment on time. I had barely sat down, when my doctor got right to the point.

"I'm sorry, but the tests indicate you have breast cancer."

Stunned, I sat in silence. My mind was at war with itself. *I'm in the best shape of my life. I run five miles a day, five times a week. I eat healthier than I ever have. What's going on? What are you talking about? What's going to happen to my son? Am I going to die?*

I was afraid, yet I kept it together because showing fear would make me look weak. Up until that day, I masked my insecurities about my upbringing and pretended to have everything together. However, control is like a house made of straw, and the minute a flame is near it can be reduced to a puff of smoke. I had come to my moment of truth without realizing it. From that day forward, I would change who I was pretending to be and reveal the imperfect, flawed, scared woman I was.

More in tune with the quick fix than with the healing process, I reviewed my options with my doctor and decided to schedule surgery. I had a month of follow-up testing, followed by two major surgeries. The first was to remove my cancerous breast and then a second surgery to create a new one. Finally, with a reconstructed breast, I was sent home to heal and get back to my life. But, things weren't going as smoothly as planned. I was having trouble. I became consumed with thoughts of *Why me? Why is this happening to me?* I tried to figure out what I could have done to have something so awful happen to me. I remember standing in the middle of my dining room and shouting at the top of my lungs, demanding that God explain to me why this was happening.

Shortly after that outburst, feeling completely out of control, I threw ten years' worth of journals into my fireplace and set them ablaze. Feeling sorry for myself, I watched them burn as I wept. It felt like I was no longer myself and that my life was over. Having left home at the age of seventeen, I had always been a controlled and independent person, but now I had to rely on other people. Having a breast removed forced me to confront my self-image, low self-esteem, and sense of low self-worth. Recovering left me exposed. I could no longer hide from myself.

Through it all, my mother was my rock. She flew from Nebraska and cared for me like only a mother knows how. Her presence was a gift. With her no-nonsense style, she brought a breath of fresh air and some sanity back to my world. Once I got home, she shined her unconditional love onto every area of my home and my healing process. We played our favorite games and watched our favorite shows. As we talked, she cooked my favorite meals, made me laugh, and most of all, let me cry.

During my mother's visit, I could feel something different happening. Not only was she helping me to physically heal, her love of me, flaws and all, helped me to release years of resentment that I hadn't consciously examined in quite some time. As I watched my mother making her famous chicken and dumplings, tears welled up in my eyes as I accepted the truth. My mother always did the best she could with what she had. The shame I carried inside about growing up fatherless and a product of the welfare system was mine to let go of, if I chose to. Finally ready to stop living my life based on the blueprint of the past, I released the shame and for the time being, borrowed some of her love to fill the empty spaces in my heart. A life-altering illness has a way of putting things into perspective like nothing else can.

After years of feeling different, awkward, and out of place, my mother's care and attention showed me just how much she loved and admired my quirky personality and zealous ambition to achieve. I finally accepted that we were alike in many ways. I stopped focusing on the negative and started paying attention to the positive. I replaced resentment and bitterness with joy. Through her love, my mother taught me to accept and trust who I was regardless of my imperfections, and that was the best gift of all.

My mom returned to Nebraska, and over the next few months, I slowly continued to heal. I had to learn to adjust, because as a woman and a mother, losing a breast created a void like losing a hand would create for a wood carpenter. I alternated between good days and tough days. I thought about what I could no longer do. For instance, if I had another child, I would only have one breast for breastfeeding, and how much my sensuality was tied to my breasts, making me feel feminine. I would sit with the pain, grieving the loss of my old identity.

I wasn't sure if I would ever get used to my new body, but I was willing to try. I welcomed the physical healing, but still avoided the mental healing because I was ashamed I was unable to immediately overcome my low self-esteem. The physical healing was actually very painful. I had to learn things like the rhythm of real patience and how to be gentle with myself. I wasn't used to doing things slowly and feeling so out of control. Having cancer and the process of putting my life back together wasn't an easy one, but I did finally start to ask questions that gave me a sense of direction and a connection to my future. I started to ask myself the big questions. Things like: "Why am I still here? Why did I survive?" and "There must be a reason my life was spared, but what is that reason?"

After everything my mother poured into me, I was devastated to find out I wouldn't have a chance to show her the rewards. I had no way of knowing the love my mother was giving me at the time of her visit was the love she so desperately needed. Diagnosed with her own aggressive form of breast cancer, my mother chose to sacrifice her pain to impart a sacrifice and love that I still carry to this day. A little over a year after my mom's return flight to Nebraska from DC, my siblings and I watched in shock at my mother's coffin being lowered into the ground as we threw the first handful of dirt into her grave.

My mother taught me that selfless sacrifice and giving could heal and change the world. She showed me this through her actions. My mother passed the torch onto me; when I give of myself, I'm giving from the gifts that my mom gave to me. A love that will heal and propel me forward is the legacy she left.

Truth be told, in the beginning, I was furious with my mother. Before she died, I had the opportunity to ask her why she didn't tell me that she also had breast cancer. Unapologetic about her decision, my mother was firm in her choices and okay with her consequences. It was difficult at first, but I learned to accept and appreciate that my mother wanted to protect the purity of her love, which was uncomplicated by the anxiety that her own diagnosis would have created had she shared it with me while I was battling my own cancer. She accepted that her life was soon going to end. She continued to give of herself, allowing laughter, good food, and tears to connect our souls forever.

The first year after my mother's death, I lived in regret. I regretted wasting so many years feeling sorry for myself and resenting my past instead of living in the present and loving my mother with my whole heart and soul. It wasn't until I acknowledged that living in regret would keep me in a life of mediocrity that I decided it was time to stand in my power in order to extend my mom's legacy from her to me, from me to my son, and from me to the world.

Surviving an illness that kills thousands of women every year can spark an awakening to wanting something more out of life. I wanted to do something meaningful with my ability to connect with people by motivating them to take action and bring their dreams to life. I learned to embrace my gift of gab. I had always been a talkative person, and I would use that gift as a speaker traveling and teaching around the country. I learned to accept my natural leadership abilities. Even in situations when I wasn't, people would often assume I was in charge. I welcomed the expansion of my gifts of vision, connection, and creativity, which I would use to build authentic lifelong relationships and support others with creating their empires. I took action towards living a spectacular life and creating a wildly successful business coaching thousands of people around the globe. Innately, I knew that right here and right now was the time for me to be and do what I was created for. I was created to be the kind of person who helped people cross over to their next level of greatness by transitioning from a life that was draining them to creating a business that gave them joy and helped them thrive. I made a decision to do the things I loved and cared about deeply, and I steered away from distractions.

I decided to walk in my power and my purpose. My journey to full purpose was unleashed when I decided to reach out to my only living parent, my absentee father. Through a series of conversations, I decided to stop living in the past and look only to what I could create in the future. I had to forgive both myself and my father. I had to be willing to no longer hold him hostage to his transgressions and instead support him in his growth. In the end, I experienced a clarity and freedom I had never experienced before. I felt whole and now had the permission I needed to move forward in my power.

I began unapologetically telling my story and inspiring others to want to do the same. I created a Reinvention Roadmap to success, detailing how I walked through my darkest hours. I began sharing it with my coaching clients and at all of my speaking events. My success steps were pinned by me as I looked back on my life and connected the dots. As excited as I was to share, I was even more excited about the progress I saw happening in my clients' lives.

Through the process of building a business, as a CEO, you have to have confidence and courage to own your failures and your successes. As I was simultaneously building my business and my confidence, I stumbled often. With an unclear brand identity, I would often attract the wrong clients. Not aware of my own brand, I would copycat others, and because it wasn't authentic to whom I was, I'd fail miserable at getting my message across to my clients and audience. When I did manage to squeak by with an unauthentic message, I was not able to get around the welfare mentality I grew up having and would undercharge for my services. Despite my failures, I kept moving forward and making the necessary changes as I pushed ahead. I eventually received coaching myself and can remember the joy and consolation of my first success when a coaching client shared with me that our work together helped her experience a mindset shift. Using the new techniques, she learned increased revenue and her self-esteem.

All my life I have been a voracious reader who loved to learn. As I studied the foundational business principles and books about consciously creating your life, I embraced the practices that gave me knowledge, and as I took action, I was able to answer my calling.

What I realized from both my failures and my successes is that I was no longer interested in looking good or impressing others. However, I was one hundred percent inspired by helping other people transform their life and business. Through dedication, self-acceptance, and commitment, I gained the courage and confidence I needed to pursue my purpose and answer my calling once and for all. I realized I was most powerful when tapping into my passion and placing faith ahead of fear. My business began to take off as I increased my expertise and worked with clients eager to change their mindset, taking their business from a dream to a reality.

In the process of working with my ideal clients, I learned how powerful our words are in creating positive mindsets. I created a series of affirmations called Mindset Mojos, a series of power thoughts and words that help us shift our mindset from negative self-chatter to empowered thinking. Instead of choosing to think positive, I was interested in choosing to BE more powerful with my thoughts and words. Each day I would say things like, "When the going gets tough, your thoughts are your most valuable resource. Not people or money. Your thoughts create your outcomes," and, "Lessons are behind me and life is what's in front of me. Now get to it!" I spoke life into my situation, and it caused me to create powerful shifts in my life and business. While healing myself, I started to share Mindset Mojo with others through social media. Mindset mojo was not only helping me, it was helping others.

My Mindset Mojo affirmations led me to the truth about myself. I was worthy of success. The only way I would live an extraordinary life and not be held hostage by the things that happened to me was to change. I was not the abandoned young girl. I was not the motherless woman. I was not a product of lack. I was no longer more interested in the past than the present. I am a woman of worth, value, integrity, and joy. My life matters, and I now use my life to serve others.

Dealing with the impact of my upbringing, I had to admit where I came from but not stay there. I let go of my old story of lack and worthlessness. I consciously made the choice to disconnect from the past script that played over and over in my mind. I learned to accept, love, and appreciate my history. I realized my upbringing was actually filled with many marvelous examples of every single skill I would use to become a successful entrepreneur. The shift to greatness began in my perception. My mother showed me what it meant to show up every day with intent on making a positive impact in the world through kindness, ingenuity, generosity, elbow grease, resilience, hard work, passion, pride, creativity, and love. As a CEO, I constantly return to the meaningful values and principles my mother taught me through her example.

I decided I had to shift my mindset from focusing on what I thought my upbringing lacked and start focusing on the abundance that was always there. I learned to take charge of my perspective and my breakthroughs, because no one else should care about my growth as much as me.

In death, my mother taught me many of the same things she had been teaching me in life, but I didn't always see the simple truth: No matter what life hands you, remember it's a gift. Our responsibility is to live life like it really matters, for one day soon it shall all come to an end.

It's been almost eight years since I began taking action and changing my mindset. Through all of my failures and successes, I have not stopped delighting and relishing in the gift of life and the magic of becoming a proud entrepreneur learning from success and failure alike. Both failure and success teaches us valuable and necessary lessons as we navigate the entrepreneurial journey. Through my journey, I have adopted several practices that contribute to my successful career as an entrepreneur. I call these eight steps my Reinvention Roadmap. The first thing I did was to create a vision. I established what I wanted. I wanted to create a future filled with authentic connections with family and friends and a business that would help thousands of women be the entrepreneurs they wanted to be. I created a plan that helped me see how I could accomplish my vision. My goals kept me on track and having a timeline of achievement created urgency. Asking for help and support kept me accountable and created invaluable community support. I intentionally made a commitment that created momentum and decided that I would no longer delay my future. Through following this roadmap, I was able to witness the manifestation of my faith. Action and faith is the legacy I choose to leave my son.

My successful secret is to walk in faith no matter how much fear shows up. I've learned that you have to put some faith with your fear, because faith will outlast fear any day. Whatever it is you desire to do consistently, choose the path of faith. Know that you don't have to get rid of fear before you take action. You are one hundred percent in charge of your future, and the faith choice never fails to be fruitful. The success you crave doesn't have to wait until you get it all together or until fear is completely erased. Your past does not dictate your future. Success is comprised of your unique process, and I encourage you to unapologetically shake up the planet by becoming the active ingredient in the fulfillment of your dream. One thing I've learned is when I choose the path of faith over fear and listen to the guidance I experience, I always prosper.

*"We are prone to judge success by the index of our salaries or the size of our automobiles rather than by the quality of our service and relationship to mankind."*

~ Martin Luther King

## Chapter 11

# LIVING IN DEPENDENCE

### Kim Fuller

My parents, sister, daughter, and I were about to pile into the oversized SUV I rented so we could ride together. As I fumbled helplessly while trying to lock my daughter's car seat in the unfamiliar car, I thought to myself, *It shouldn't be this hard. Where is the darn latch?* I could feel their eyes beaming through the back of my head as frustration set in. Nobody spoke and nobody stepped in to help. I knew they wanted to, but they were frozen in their inability to offer and I was frozen in my inability to ask. They were probably afraid I was going to blow up at them.

*He would know how to help me, I thought. But he isn't here. He's not coming back.* Then it hit me like a ton of bricks. *He's gone and this is how it's going to be from now on, me and my daughter against the world with only each other to depend on.* This was the moment I realized my husband was indeed gone forever. It was also a major turning point in my life and the reason why I became the entrepreneur I am today.

As a mother, I work hard every day to let my daughter know she can depend on me. As a life coach, I want my clients to do the same. As a small business owner, I know I can't make a living without the vendors and clients who help me grow my business. However, when I was younger and prior to being married, my definition of success was rooted in my own individual achievement. I thought that meant I had to be focused—and be independent. I'm a little embarrassed to admit it now, but I never wanted to depend on anyone and certainly didn't expect to have anyone depend on me. That mindset spilled over into my personal life. I dated, but I didn't really think I would find someone who was on the same page as me. I was okay with that because I had no plans to take care of somebody's household, children, or pets.

Then Charles happened. And wouldn't you know, he was just like me. We enjoyed being together, but enjoyed our own space. He, too, had no plans to take care of somebody's house, children, or pets. Part of our lifestyle involved traveling the world and taking active vacations each year, enjoying many adventures—skiing, sailing, snorkeling, shopping, whatever suited our fancy.

I was committed to being independent. Therefore, I didn't reach out to ask for assistance. There were times when I just bit my tongue in frustration and anger, confused because I needed to reach out and talk to someone and share all of these sudden life changes and challenges. I isolated myself by trying to manage Charles' illness and my work stress alone.

My work also started to suffer. Offered a promotion to senior mental health director at my job, I jumped at the opportunity for more responsibility and more money. Feeling stuck and stagnant, I thought this opportunity would give me a much-needed jumpstart. Charles grew sicker, had contracted pneumonia, and was in and out of the emergency room. The fallout with my job happened when I wasn't able to live up to some of my new obligations. Add to that the fact I couldn't tell my boss what was going on because I had committed myself to Charles' secret. Within a few weeks, I was demoted back to my old position. However, I was too engrossed in Charles' needs to experience or acknowledge my shame and defeat.

Although trained well to do my job as a mental health director, I wasn't confident I was actually helping people move from feeling overwhelmed and oppressed to empowered and productive. The truth is, I was searching for that myself. I was eager to find something that would lift me out of the drudgery of commuting and propel me into a life in which I felt I had more control, one that was predictable and would allow me to continue to travel whenever I wanted to. But, try as I might, I couldn't figure it out myself.

I shared my needs, desires, and wants when I finally confided in my very good friend Terri, and she suggested I talk with her sister who was a life coach. My conversations with Carrie were very encouraging and enthusiastic. She helped me see how being a life coach could become a real possibility. I wanted to work with clients who desired self-growth. So, I worked at setting up a five-year plan for me to transition out of my job and into being a life coach. We even came up with a name and menu of services for my potential new business: Fuller Life Concepts. When I did establish the business, I kept the name and now offer many of the same services we discussed, including Life Coaching and Business Coaching.

After I made the decision, the challenge then became how to actually do it. I was still working at my 9-to-5 job, which I needed for financial reasons. While home on maternity leave, I continued to plan out how I would pursue life coaching even further. I saw it as a way to be closer to home, allowing me to make a living while still be an attentive wife and mother to my husband and child.

Charles' dependency on me became more complicated. We decided to get away for a ski weekend in Mammoth, California. The sun had already set, and bordered by white mounds of snow, the road looked like it had been parted for us. Charles had been complaining of fatigue and swollen glands; he'd recently had a doctor's appointment and was sharing the results. I looked at his profile as he spoke, listening intently as he reported the results of his tests. They were positive for excessive white blood cells, a type of leukemia. I continued to stare at his profile, not fully understanding the gravity of his words as he calmly announced that his doctors said it would take a fatal toll within about ten years. The car was as silent and calm inside as it appeared outside, except I was screaming inside. Charles decided he would try to have a full, independent life in the short time he had left. Not wanting pity, he didn't tell anyone about his diagnosis and swore me to secrecy. I couldn't tell my family, friends, or my boss. It was our big secret.

The day I wrestled with the carseat was the day of Charles' funeral. It seems to stand as the demarcation between my first life, as someone who clung to independence, and the life I live today—as a mom and entrepreneur who embraces dependence. Here's why. During this time, I was very aware that I would at some point be a solo parent and that my beautiful little girl would be depending on me. Her dependence made me dependable. So, I took on the task of getting certified as a professional life coach. It was becoming more urgent for me to get more control over my life.

I left my job eight weeks after the funeral. I had an epiphany and realized I needed my village in order to cope. At the time, I didn't recognize it was dependence, but there were people who I knew would rally around my need for support. I learned this lesson acutely as I struggled alone with Charles' illness. Charles was in and out of chemotherapy treatments and had to get blood transfusions at times. There were many doctor and hospital visits, but nobody knew. When others depend on us, it makes us dependable. Knowing my clients need my expertise to help them achieve their goals makes me want to live up to the promise.

My transition from someone who valued independence above all else, to someone who recognizes dependence as a business asset is one of those journeys that's perhaps the greatest learning experience of my life, especially when you consider all the mental and psychological shifts I made to get where I am. From the outside looking in, it may have looked as if I was handling everything with grace and ease, but I wasn't. The challenge of going through the grief process with a newborn child, starting a new business, and trying to manage all of the affairs was very overwhelming. The pressure of having to do it all on my own was sometimes flattening. It felt like a great time for me to separate from being a full-time employee and jump right into full-time life coaching. That was a good and bad decision. I didn't technically have enough clients to live on the income from my coaching. So, I took on contract positions, which I call bridge or stopgap jobs. I could have gotten another full-time job where I would have a stable income, two weeks of vacation, and other benefits. However, the last five years have been the most monumental in terms of the life changes and business milestones that have occurred.

Looking back on the journey, I realize my two biggest struggles were overcoming loneliness—both working as a solopreneur and in managing my pain and grief—and becoming comfortable with my identity as an entrepreneur. Once I let myself embrace dependence, I was better able to tackle both of these obstacles.

After my husband's death, I was told I was courageous and strong. It felt awkward to admit that I was feeling less than brave and that I was lonely and uncertain about the decisions I was making. I was exploding on people, losing weight, and crying often. I was stressed and struggling financially, wondering how could I take on more work with an infant. The pressure to get more clients, make more money, and create a lucrative business was immense pressure that I thought I had under control.

On Mother's Day, I ran to the store for a few items for dinner and saw a sea of daddies with their children buying cards and flowers for moms. I thought, *My daughter will never have this experience with her daddy.* With tears rolling down my cheeks, I purchased the few items; the cashier kindly offered me a tissue without a word. I had yelled at my mom for asking how I was doing when I walked in and slammed the door so hard the house rattled. Her response, "You should talk to someone." Later that same month, a friend pulled me aside and asked in "that" tone, "How are you doing? Are you seeing anyone?" I finally got the message; I acquiesced and contacted a grief-and-loss coach who specializes in working with grief after losing someone to cancer. By unleashing the burden of secrecy to people who wanted to help me, I was able to get out of the lonely place I sought refuge.

Soon after starting my business, whenever someone asked what I do for a living, I found myself stuttering and responding with my old identity of being in non-profit mental health. This was comfortable, pre-programmed, and easy. I had not fully accepted the identity of Life Coach Entrepreneur and Business Owner. Moreover, I felt if I admitted that I was a fledgling businessperson, they wouldn't take me seriously. I would find myself at networking meetings answering the question regarding what I do with something like this, "Well, I am a director of…well, I'm a life coach…well, I'm a…I'm a… I'm a…" And just not having the words. I remember when people asked me about my marital status. I would be like, "I'm ah…a wi (stuttering)…I'm not married." The only thing I knew for sure was that I was the mother of a beautiful, healthy baby girl. So, I never hesitated to brag about her and show pictures. Without intending to, I had created an icebreaker. This beautiful little girl who was depending on me to do well at providing for her was allowing me to connect with others in spite of myself. I guess you can say I was also depending on her.

However, I realized I had to start living in my new identity in order to succeed. Before my first networking meeting, I sent an email to the organizer. He replied, "Bring business cards to share." The process of getting to a breakfast meeting was taxing. I had to ask for help to leave home at 6:30 a.m., but not before nursing my daughter. Then I shedded tears from being overwhelmed and feeling rushed on the drive there.

At the meeting, we had some casual networking time that I also used to run to the restroom so I could check to make sure there was no mascara smudges from the tears. When I sat down to breakfast, the organizer announced it was time for 60-second introductions.

*Guests go first? What! I just arrived at this and now have to get up and do a commercial about my business?*

I stuttered and stammered through the first "commercial" introduction. I could have left in shame and never returned. Instead, I did this over and over again every week for a year, allowing myself to be vulnerable, and showing I needed help earned me advice. The tenacity I showed by working at it every week earned me respect. My reward was that I became increasingly comfortable with my identity, business strategy, business management, and how to give and receive referrals for business. This experience is what really made me comfortable at networking. Now I attend about four or five different network groups each month.

First, identify what you need. I didn't know what I needed, and it took friends and family members to point out that I was exploding everywhere. Next, identify specific people to support you in specific tasks that will encourage you to build certain skill sets. My mother was great at babysitting her granddaughter and offering emotional support and encouragement.

She wouldn't have done as well in advising me on tax planning. Everyone in my village had a specific role, and I knew I could call on them for that specific task if I needed to. When a situation came up, I didn't have to wonder how I would deal with it; I had experts to call on. My business coach and mentor, my family, grief-and-loss coach, and numerous people I met through networking became mentors, helping me figure out how to confront business situations. I asked a colleague about contract work for extra money. I used online babysitter sites and always have three to four sitters on call, especially for those evening business-related events.

As I think back, there was a specific assignment my grief counselor gave me that helped me break through a lot of the fear and shame I was experiencing. I had to share my whole story with a friend, specifically someone who did not know my story. I was terrified, so worried about rejection, about judgment, about having to manage their feelings. (I'm a therapist, so I'm always prepared to manage others' feelings.) I was trembling and sweating during the discussion (monologue). The response was loving and warm. I felt accepted.

My successful secret is to use your resources and ask for help. I believed asking for help meant that I was incapable, limited, and ineffective. What I've learned is that asking for what you need is empowering and gratifying. One of my favorite quotes by Brene Brown is, "When you cannot accept and ask for help without self-judgment, then when you offer other people help, you are always doing so with judgment." People struggle with asking because of judgment and shame. Asking is necessary with building a business. You have to identify the people who can help you cope with loneliness. Mine was double fisted: the loneliness of being a solopreneur and a widow. Those were two very new identities I needed to become comfortable with. It doesn't mean that I no longer value (even enjoy) independence. Now, I enjoy living my life in dependence of my supporters.

*"The key to realizing a dream is to focus not on success but significance — and then even the small steps and little victories along your path will take on greater meaning."*

~ Oprah Winfrey

# Chapter 12

# READY TO FACE FEAR: JUST DO IT!

## LeShawnda Fitzgerald

At the age of nineteen, I dropped out of college to support my daughter shortly after her birth. I knew having an education would improve our lives, but at the time, I needed to be a woman, support her, and sadly put my dreams on hold. As I entered the workforce full-time, I knew there was more to living than working a nine-to-five for the rest of my life. I had goals and dreams that I wanted to pursue. I just wasn't sure how I was going to make them come true.

*Just Do It!* These were the words running through my mind. I knew if I began thinking too hard, I might talk myself out of listening to that little voice screaming for me to buck the traditional nine-to-five success model. It had been ingrained in me that security, safety, and responsibility came from going to college, working that perfect job, and buying the house with the white picket fence. So, I was terrified of walking away from everything I had come to know as normal. My goal now was to believe that I could "Just Do It!" While weighing the pros and cons of starting my own business, I was afraid of the impact a change in finances and politics might have on my family and moreso on myself. However, that inner spirit began to resonate and I knew I had to take a chance on me.

I have always wanted to start my own business. As a little girl, ideas and concepts came easy to me. I was the person trying to figure out how to take simple notions and make them bigger, different, or mine. I love and appreciate walking in the park and watching the dandelion petals blow in the wind. The peace I felt from creating art in my mind by rearranging the clouds gave me the hope I needed to make it through day-by-day. I attribute my creative drive to being an enthusiastic learner and passionate teacher. I have bathed in the sunshine and taken shelter from thunderstorms. I have loved until my head hurts and felt pain that no prescription could heal.

Over the course of my life, I have worked many jobs in hopes that I would find my niche – find that fulfillment I heard so much about. But, it was so befitting that my perfect fit would be birthed from the deep-rooted inspiration I would mold with my own hands.

It is definitely true when they say it takes a village. I had a strong community of women who hungrily shared their lessons learned, and as if I was famished, I ated it all up. These teachings encouraged me to seek what I had left behind and to re-enroll in college. I looked to faith to get me through because I believed God would make a way out of no way. While working a part-time job and going to school, I was blessed to have a grandmother who watched my daughter, cooked for us, gave me money when I came up short, believed in my gifts, and encouraged me when I needed it. With the love and support of my family and friends, I completed college with a degree in Spanish and History and was immediately accepted into graduate school. I was very proud of the legacy I was starting for me and my daughter.

Upon getting my undergrad degree, I took a job as a Spanish teacher. It was horrible ! I had no idea what I was doing. My classes were overflowing, and I did not earn the respect from my students. In turn, they had no interest in learning Spanish. During this time, I felt like I was hanging on a flimsy limb. My school's administrative staff and fellow co-workers were also overwhelmed. I was in graduate school full time with so many deadlines I could not keep up, and I was the sole provider for my daughter. However, at this point, my misery was not important. I know now this experience was part of God's plan to prepare me for the biggest shift to my forthcoming reality, because at the end of the school year I was let go. I was both scared and relieved.

No matter the circumstance, we have to take a moment to celebrate our blessings. During this time of great stress, my grandmother, who was my backbone, was battling terminal cancer, and I found myself in a whirlwind of emotion. I was thankful for being able to embrace the wisdom she shared, but I also questioned God, as my selfishness could not imagine my lifeline no longer in my world. I found myself in a cyclical pattern of dissatisfaction with my teaching career and once again pregnant with my second child without a partner to support me or my unborn son.

Overwhelmed with the thought of having to raise two children alone, I started calling daily meetings with God. I spoke to him about my vision and set out to make it plain. I knew for certain I wanted to have an active part in my children's day-to-day activities. I did not want any parts of a life where I was too exhausted to experience the beauty of motherhood. I knew I did not want to return to teaching after I had my son. The thought of being too tired to spend time with my children made me sink to a place of darkness, causing my body to become lifeless. Wanting a change, I begged to be let off of this merry-go-round.

My daily sessions started to payoff. The Lord spoke a new existence in me. I recall telling my best friend at the time that after my delivery, I wanted to stay home with the kids. She laughed and sarcastically asked, "How are you going to do that?" I sat with her words for a while. I knew we were in a recession, but I also knew I had the perfect One in my corner and He could do anything. I still harbored doubt, but my mustard seed of faith and desire to stay home with my children was the remedy I needed to start restoration.

Rebuilding did not come how I had envisioned it initially, but I made the best of it. I was laid off from my job at the end of that academic year, which I viewed as progression. (At least this time I was not fired.) I took it as a sign and began focusing on the upcoming birth of my son. While mulling over my situation, I had an idea that I could teach Spanish classes at my church, which would allow me to spend the majority of my time with my children. I now had a Bachelors, two Masters, and was working toward a Doctoral degree. I had come a long way, and I knew I definitely had the qualifications. In addition, I had two years of experience teaching urban students and overcoming challenging classroom conditions.

Over the course of one week, I created some flyers, business cards, and a website. I reached out to my network, and the following month I began offering two Spanish classes a week to children in a classroom at church. Those two classes quickly grew to four classes a week. Then we added adult classes and summer Spanish camp. The program grew so quickly that the church no longer wanted to house the program, which left me a short time to find an independent space. Doors opened for me, and a space became available. I could not really afford it, but I trusted that things would work themselves out. We outgrew our first location in six months and moved to our current location. What started as a way to stay home with my children has grown into an independent language learning center that uses my passion for teaching to enhance children's and adult's knowledge of Spanish language and culture.

The success of my company, Ready for Spanish, did not happen overnight. Nor has the journey to entrepreneurship been easy. There have been many challenges, limited monies, and overdue bills. In addition, I was coping with the loss of my grandmother who passed away only days after I gave birth to my son. But, I believed I was only in the beginning of my destiny. I stepped out on faith to start something great.

In all honesty, fear was a factor throughout my letdowns and my wins. When I began my business, I did not have start-up money saved nor the credit score needed to obtain a business loan. As a result, I began questioning myself. There was so much at stake. What if I could not balance it all? I was struggling, and my fear was seeping out of the cracks like water in a flooded basement. I wasn't taking care of myself physically or mentally. I would sometimes go days without eating or sleeping. I stopped going out with friends. My sole priorities were caring for my children and growing my business; these two things consumed my being. I quickly burned out and was losing what I needed to pull through. My business, although steady, was not at the level I wanted it to be. It seemed like the harder I pushed forward, the more failure pushed back. I put in more effort than I had ever produced in my life, yet money wasn't my reward. I wanted to know what was truly standing in my way, and I was going to figure it out.

I needed help. I had never really asked for help before. I took on the role of supermom and superwoman, but in reality, I could not fly alone. My daughter was old enough to help around the house. I also hired someone to come in and clean our home bi-weekly. Doing the laundry once per week was excruciating for me, so I taught my daughter how to do her own laundry and gave her a laundry day. Once my home was running smoothly, it helped me to relax as I conducted my daily business affairs.

I had no prior experience running a business, but I knew there were changes I had to make if I was going to continue on this path. First, I had to make a choice: faith or fear? Although I had heard it before, I knew at this point faith and fear could not reside together. Faith requires action. Fear leaves us immobile. To go forward, I needed to eliminate fear from my life. I needed to completely transform my thinking and eliminate thoughts, people, and things that were holding me back. This was a bold move, but being an entrepreneur requires courage and faith. Thus, the transformation began.

Somewhere along the way I forgot about my greatness and what I was meant to do. I thought I could fake it until I made it. However, faking it only resulted in me being pulled further from my goals. I got caught up in keeping up appearances. Buying designer clothes and cars that I could not afford. I got caught up in people pleasing and was more concerned with gaining love and approval from others. I got into the habit of seeking advice verses listening to the Word. It was easier to follow other people's plan for my life than for me to listen to my inner spirit. I wondered what others would think and if I would have their support. Although I was afraid of being alone, it was exactly what I needed. I needed time to find myself, learn how to trust within, seek divine wisdom, and follow spiritual guidance. It was time for me to get serious, to grow, and to face my trepidation.

Each day as my faith grew, I became stronger, more confident, and wiser. I was able to tune out distractions and focus on my end goals. I no longer felt the need to seek out approval from others. I learned how to approve of myself, so I didn't crave acceptance from anyone else. I did not have to distress about the unknown because I accepted that my future was bright.

As a single mom, I had to realize I was not alone. I trusted that the good people who wanted the very best for my children and me would be there. I sought out time to just breathe and pray, to regroup and refocus. In preparation, I found confidence. No one can block me unless I give them permission or I choose to give away my power. I began to live shamelessly and deliberately. I was no longer faking it. I was "faithing" it, and things began to move on my behalf.

As my business continued to progress, I took some time to evaluate what was working. For the first time in my life, work didn't feel like labor. "Ready for Spanish" represented the perfect balance of who I am. Growth didn't always mean compensation. I responsibly cut my expenses in order to sustain my household. I did not always enjoy the process. So, I posted a *Beware of Pitfall* sign in my memory bank to remind me to continue submitting to my development, knowing I will be taken care of. I remembered not to spend valuable energy focused on what was going wrong instead of all that I had done right. I needed to live my dreams through the right lenses. My perspective of my circumstances was critical to the manifestation of my vision. I had to stop complaining. I had to speak greatness into the universe, and I had to believe in what I did not know. I always knew what I wanted. Now it was time for me to act and think accordingly. I knew without a doubt that I could do it, that I could be a successful entrepreneur, and that I did not have to sacrifice my children. I knew I could be happy, at peace, and have all the desires of my heart. I trusted myself, walked in faith, and knew God would handle the rest. So, it was done.

I followed my heart and stayed home with my son until he began school. My desire to stay home and build a career that allowed me to focus on my children is not foreign; it is something all single mothers can do. If you have a vision, own it, believe it can happen, act on faith, know that you are supported, and watch it all come to fruition. My initial act of faith was returning to college after having my daughter. I then leaped when I started my business by creating a simple flyer advertising my classes. I have found there is power in moving beyond the first step of idea to action.

Don't allow the many tasks of parenthood keep you from starting your business. As a single mom, there will always be things that need to be done. Implement a system that works for your family by giving your children more responsibilities or call upon friends and family to help you where needed.

I also suggest surrounding yourself with people who encourage and support you. When you are on the road to something great, there will be naysayers. They will have millions of reasons why you cannot or should not step out on your own. You have options. Love them and ignore them or leave them. Do not get caught up in their disbelief. This is your dream, not theirs. Do not let others deter you from the greatness that is in store for you.

When things get rough, do not be afraid. Do not give up. Even when things seem hard and you are clueless as to what is taking place, have peace in knowing this is a preparation period and everything will work out for your good. Stay strong in you. Do not compare yourself to anyone.

Being a business owner has reminded me of who I am and the power within and around me. I am no longer afraid to ask for help when I need it. I have learned to forgive, to let go, to love and accept myself unconditionally. I am still in the process of releasing limitations I have placed, and my challenge has been to get out of my own way by releasing any fears that may be blocking me and act on my beliefs. I am not afraid to be myself. That is the only way I can live *my* dreams. Entrepreneurship taught me accountability. I am accountable for what I do, say, and think. If I fall short or stand tall, it is all due to the actions I take, and I have learned how to roll with the highs and the lows.

My successful secret is to trust and be kind to yourself. Do not beat yourself up over mistakes or what seem to be setbacks. I now realize mistakes are a necessary part of the growth and learning process. I surrender to this process because I have experienced God's provision, omnipresence, and I am in tune with the light within myself to bring forth my dreams. Because of this, as a single mompreneur, I am not alone. I am secure; I am empowered; I walk in purpose and know I can do all things. It wasn't until after my faith journey that I learned to depend on a source much greater than myself or any man. You, too, have access to this power. Wherever you are in your entrepreneurial pursuits, focus on your goals, declare your success, follow your heart, trust the process, and know that everything is working out for your greatest good.

*"Success is just a war of attrition. Sure, there's an element of talent you should probably possess. But, if you just stick around long enough, eventually something is going to happen."*

~Dax Shepard

## Chapter 13

# EMBRACING YOUR UNIQUENESS: LEARNING TO WALK IN YOUR PURPOSE GOD'S WAY

### Jennifer Fontanilla

Throughout my earlier years, dreaming of lofty goals with the intent of checking them off my "to-do" list was a common practice. Many nights, my husband and I sat dreaming about the countries that would be stamped on the pages of our passports or sucking up the courage to do adventurous activities that would make our hearts pump with adrenaline. We were best friends, business partners, and so in love. Therefore, when my little utopian world began to crumble, being faced with the reality of starting life all over again without him forced me to view the world and how I operated in it with only one set of eyes. After almost a decade of looking out for the two of us, I was now going to have to plan things solo. The energy, excitement, and drive left my body, and I looked for ways to physically and mentally escape in order to cope and make it through one more day.

In the midst of trying to forget about all the pain and lost memories, I found myself pregnant. Why was this happening to me now? I didn't plan this. I didn't want kids yet! (Did I even want them?) I was busier than ever with trying to rebuild my business and get it off the ground. More disappointment set in, and I felt as if nothing was going right anymore.

I shook my head while thinking, *Why is it I can help others when it comes to their personal and financial problems, including giving them advice regarding what to invest in, but I can't seem to get my own head straight? What the heck is wrong with me?* So much for that perfect life I was trying to create. I almost felt worried and sad for my unborn child. What kind of a mother was he going to have? All I could associate myself with was failure.

I like to tell people I've used all sides of my brain. I originally started off wanting to be a doctor, but couldn't ignore the creative side I possessed. It was a progression of working at a local print shop, to an entry-level job for the Yellow Pages, to being asked to be a co-owner of that same print shop, to becoming a long-term freelance designer. Within that short period of time, I learned how to create my own hours, demand my own pay, and get a taste of what it would be like to be my own boss. Although incredibly talented at what I did, I felt an internal emptiness. I wanted to feel like I was truly impacting people's lives.

While sitting in my little design room at work staring at my computer monitor, I reflected on all the money I was making and thought to myself, *I have no idea if what I'm doing with my money is the best thing possible. I didn't learn anything in school on how to handle this part of my adult life. Why wasn't I taught how to save other than just opening up a checking account at the bank down the street? What are mutual funds and stocks? How can I learn about investments? Were my parents supposed to educate me on this? I bet I'm losing out on many opportunities simply because of a lack of knowledge."*

I began to get frustrated. I hated feeling any void, and the fact that this had an immense impact on my future began to stir something within me. I couldn't be the only one wondering.

Here I was taking a massive leap of faith. I had no idea how I was going to do it or if it would even work. All I knew was at that very moment, I made a decision to enter an entirely different industry and help others with their lack of knowledge regarding what they should be doing when it came to their money. If people weren't going to be shown the way, they needed someone to hold their hand and help them make smart financial decisions. Before my son came along, I was a free spirit. All I thought about was how

I would make money for my business and the next fun thing to do on my list of adventures. That all came to a screeching halt the day I went into labor; everything changed.

I thank God that my mother, who is a complete blessing, had been retired for a few years at this point and was gracious enough to help me. She stepped up to the plate and watched the baby for me while I worked and did whatever I needed to do. I didn't really take any time off from work. After all, if you stop, everything else stops.

Your world is no longer about you. Your time is no longer just yours. Your money is no longer about what you need or want. Adjusting my time has been my biggest challenge by far. Networking and events have become a big struggle, as well, in terms of deciding whether it is good for my business, especially when many of them are held at night and run late. At the beginning of every week, I print out my schedule for my mom so she'll know when I need her help. I now have to calculate driving time, how long I'll stay at an event or appointment, and when to leave in order to be back home by a certain time. These things were not issues before, but now with a child, I had to think about these things. Attending workshops and conferences are even bigger hurdles because it sometimes requires me to travel out of state and be gone for days

When you're single, there's no second income or husband to help financially support your dreams while you're trying to build your empire. There is no tag-teaming and planning whose turn it is to watch your child. You're on a constant hustle trying to make it on your own for you and your child and figuring out how to make the dream of having your own business happen no matter what. Sure, you can get help from loved ones around you, but at the end of the day, it's all your responsibility and your job to figure out how you're going to masterfully orchestrate this circus act.

The days of thinking you'll tackle any unfinished business when you get home is a laughable intention. I know the minute I step into the house and my little hurricane is in full-swing, there is no catching up on anything. I have literally sat in my driveway for up to an hour making last-minute phone calls because it has evolved into my quiet fortress of solitude with no interruptions or screams for attention from my child. It is during these times I know I am developing more character and patience. Trust me, I've had my share of hair pulling (my own, of course), eye rolling, and sighs. That's when you need to just breathe, breathe, and breathe some more while repeating this mantra that has been instilled within me: "It's only for a season." This is the reality of juggling motherhood and entrepreneurship, especially when you are on your own.

However, challenges come with lessons, and you learn to develop a different perspective on life. Although it may sometimes feel as if I've lost my freedom, being a mother has been an absolute blessing and given me ultimate joy. It is something about being a mother that gives you a different drive and another level of motivation for your business. I had to learn how to slow down, be unselfish of myself and of my time. Time management has become more important than ever.

I look forward to the days when my hard work will pay off. My dreams are what keep me focused on why I am doing all of this. I want to be able to give my son so much and not come from a mentality of lack, but rather that of abundance. I'm learning and practicing how to balance my time with my son and with my business. When the days are tough and I'm on my last bit of energy, I am reminded by his Kool-Aid smile that I should treasure these moments. He will not be this tender age forever, and I want to be able to enjoy all his tiny idiosyncrasies. Does that mean I don't miss all the fun I used to have? Absolutely not. However, I am in a different place right now. My priorities are focused on him and my business, but I do make sure that every once in awhile I do something fun for myself. Being an entrepreneur has forced me to make my own decisions and schedule, and although there is no guaranteed paycheck and benefits, for me, there is no comparison to having the ability to dictate how to grow my business.

There came a point in my career in the financial services industry where I felt lost and apathetic. I would complain to myself when things weren't going right. I started to doubt my abilities and myself. I constantly questioned whether or not I was cut out for this. No matter how many accolades I received from numerous colleagues and clients or how many times I was invited to be a guest speaker for various events, the nagging voice of doubt within would get the best of me. Worst of all, I was guilty of comparing myself to others who did the same type of work. I started to feel inadequate when looking at their websites, established social media outlets, and many letters of credentials after their name. Like an ungrateful brat, I would whine, "Well, they have a supportive husband/partner" or "They're single and have more time to do all that." I felt myself being emotionally drawn into a downward spiral.

It was time to open up and get some insight. A dear friend and business coach, whom I adore, took some time to analyze what I was going through. She told me one simple thing: "You are enough. You are so ready." It was so simple, yet powerful. There was no need for all that madness!

I read the Bible every day, prayed, and studied scriptures on God's word and how business professionals can apply it in all aspects of their work. In Psalm 139:13, it says, *"For you created my inmost being; you knit me together in my mother's womb."* I forgot how unique I am and what I offer to others that they cannot get anywhere else. The other scripture that has been my foundation is Jeremiah 29:11, *"For I know the plans I have for you,"* declared the LORD. *"Plans to prosper you and not to harm you; plans to give you hope and a future."* God made me refocus on every aspect of what was going on in my business so I could be grateful for the person that He made me to be. This enabled me to become the person He wants me to be, not someone else.

I had to shut up and take responsibility. I had to figure out my schedule, my time management, and accept that I am pretty much doing this on my own with some help and to make the most of the resources around me. I was called to help others, and the only way I could be useful is if I started to focus and get serious about what I was doing.

The biggest challenge I am still learning to overcome is that I am not in control. I had to learn to surrender to God, His plans, and His timing. The more I have learned to do this, the lighter the load feels. I've noticed that I am now slow to anger, my frustration dissipates, and I feel comforted when I lean on what I know He has in store for my son and me.

Be forewarned that not everyone, including friends and family, will always be supportive. In fact, sometimes they can be the biggest naysayers. And that's okay. No, it doesn't mean they're bad people, but I quickly learned that sometimes we have to separate our goals and dreams from certain people because it simply is not the world they operate within. The world of entrepreneurship is a far cry from someone who is comfortable working for someone else. So, make sure to form your "go-to team" of positive and uplifting people who can continue to encourage and support you. You will need people in your life that you can bounce ideas off of or just to be your soundboard when you want to cry when things fall through, such as having a horrible faux pas with a client.

Remember to make time for yourself each day by reading your favorite book for fifteen minutes, taking a short walk for lunch, or having coffee with a close friend. For me, my outlet and "mom-me time" is working out. I go every morning and great ideas seem to gravitate towards me. It keeps my mind alert. I do it after I pray and meditate. When we don't allow ourselves to do this, we go nuts and burn out. Don't feel guilty, because it is not selfish. Selfish behavior can sometimes be neglecting yourself, because if you cannot function, what good are you to yourself, your business, and your child?

Another way to start manifesting your entrepreneurial dreams is to immerse yourself in constant learning. I subscribe to many business coaches' newsletters and many offer free teleseminars. Ask people within your network who they like to follow, and soon enough, you should have hours of listening. Be sure to find out what conferences, workshops, or seminars are being held within your area. It is always best to bring a friend along, but make it a point to set a number of how many new connections you'll have by the end of the event. This will help you build up your confidence and network of contacts.

Each day give yourself the gift of time, whether it is to meditate and connect with God or whatever higher being you believe in. From a mental and health standpoint, doing this will help you stay grounded and more focused. If you're constantly running around like a headless chicken, what kind of results do you think your business is going to create? Whether you meditate or just want to journal, allow yourself some time to think each day out and plan your actions. Always focus on how you want to feel with every decision you make. What is the outcome and feeling associated with it that you want to experience? Does it serve a purpose for what you are working towards? Remember, your time is precious. For example, does working with a particular client bring you joy or do you cringe when you see their number show up on your phone? Understand why you take the actions you do.

Think about what you are grateful for and develop ways you can show that gratitude extended beyond just thinking about it. Can you help someone's cause or donate your time? Can you help someone set up their workshop or promote it for them? By doing these things, you can find a way to give back to others and pay it forward. Ensure that you have an attitude of gratitude. It does incredible wonders for your soul and well-being.

Find a higher purpose behind the money. There's nothing wrong with wanting to make bazillions, but what is it all for? You need to discover your purpose and drive; otherwise, it will be all in vain.

Finally, be excited about YOUR journey, even if you are venturing off on your own. Embrace the fear and get comfortable with it. Don't be afraid of failure or taking chances. If all else fails, you will recover from it and come out stronger, wiser, and more brilliant.

My successful secret is simply trusting God and knowing that He is ahead of you leading your steps and behind you to catch you when you fall. Many leaders in the Bible went out to battle, even when they doubted their capabilities, and only by the grace and hand of God were they able to overcome all obstacles and challenges. As entrepreneurs, we endure failures and tough situations because God brings you these challenges to prepare you for something bigger. In the end, you are stronger and ready to take on more as you continue on your journey of fulfilling your dreams. Have faith, be open to what God will provide for you, and praise Him when it happens. Sow seeds of gratefulness to reap more doors of opportunities. Seek His wisdom and guidance while knowing that He wants you to be successful and prosperous. With Him, everything is possible.

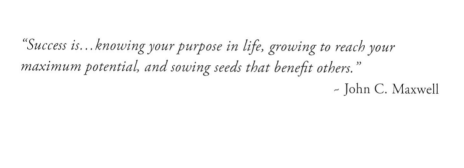

*"Success is…knowing your purpose in life, growing to reach your maximum potential, and sowing seeds that benefit others."*

~ John C. Maxwell

## Chapter 14

# PLAY TO WIN: BET ON YOURSELF

## Kiana Shaw

Whenever I see expressions of love, my heart skips a beat at my memories of being loved and of loving. I have found there is nothing like those first moments of new love. The time when you tell your girlfriends about the hope of him, or when you secretly practice writing your first name with his last name. There are not enough words to describe the memory of his hand running across the small of your back as he guides you to the other side of the street. Love, my friend, can be so very rich, but it can also force us into a deep reflection when it goes bad.

I have learned that my love is not thin. I would give all of me in hopes of getting all of him. It may not seem logically to some, but I learned at a very early age that love is in our actions; it is what we do and say to the people whom we profess to love. However, after some valleys and hills, life has taught me to love me first, and in loving me, I can love him better. I was not always in a space where I knew or understood the power of loving me.

I can recall the day I learned of his affair like it was yesterday. I was sitting in my car with the radio just above a whisper as I listened to my distant cousin confirm their two-year relationship. As her passionate words came fast and hard, my mind darted in and out of our four years of loving, planning, and building. With all of me, I believed he and I had established a foundation that was destined for the chapel. On the surface, I was mad to the point where I was seeing red, but if I am to be honest, I was hurt, embarrassed, and ashamed for loving him so blindly and me so little. It was in that moment of mixed emotions that I decided I would empower other women to love themselves first and in essence live for themselves. Although I had these thoughts, I knew I needed to receive this message just as much as I needed to deliver it.

I am better today than I was yesterday; and I will be better tomorrow than I am today because I have found the strength to fight for me and to campaign for women loving the core of who they are and what they desire to become. There comes a time in our lives when we are forced to sit back and evaluate the people, choices, and mistakes we have made. This process is never easy because it requires us to be honest with ourselves, not the neatly packaged person that we present to the world. But, when we have put our masks in the wash and turned the cycle to hot, our calling and purpose will shine so brightly that we will be saddened it took us so long to put ourselves in the machine. As a single mother, my goal is to ensure that my daughter does not endure the same type of pain I have experienced, because not only is it my business as a coach to teach young women to love themselves, it is my duty to teach my daughter the same when she becomes a young woman.

It is funny to think that when we are young we believe we can do anything, but as we grow and life begins to throw us curve balls, we no longer dream. Instead, we look for safety, which is one of the worst things we can do to ourselves. Those who know me would classify me as a fun-loving, energetic, and kind person. I am usually the individual spreading the happy juice, but one morning while driving to work, I could not manage to keep a smile on my face. My mind was asking questions that my heart was not ready to process, let alone answer. So, I being human tried to silence myself. I began to play gospel music in hopes that my thoughts would be redirected, but this did nothing for me. I even tried listening to my favorite hardcore rap songs. You know, the ones that force you to curse and dance like you're in the house alone, but nothing. My inner voice would not be silenced.

As I turned into the parking lot of my job, I was overwhelmed with emotions and began to sob. Between moments of uncontrollable shaking, snot dripping from my nose, my pounding on the steering wheel, and brushing away the river of tears gliding down my face, I cried out to God. I knew in my heart that my life was more than a traditional nine-to-five. For the first time in a long while, I allowed myself to speak life over me and into me as I prayed, *God, I know you have more for me than this! I want more, Lord. I need more! I cannot keep coming to this job knowing that you have chosen me to do more and be better than I am. Lord, I need you to help me reach my calling.*

Two years prior to this moment, I started a foundation called Village of Truth. When I started this venture, I was dedicated to creating a healthy outlet for teenager girls to build their self-esteem, participate in career building activities, and become voices for their communities. However, life took over and I spent more time focused on working for a company that was considered one of the best 100 companies to work for. Ironically, I hated my job. It was not a good fit. It was challenging for me to adjust to their micro- management style. After some time with the company, I was informed I was being let go, which was a nice way of saying, "You're fired." The normal protocol for this moment would dictate that I should cry, be sad, and question my ability, but instead, I was happy. I walked out the meeting excited about the unemployment I would collect while building my foundation.

Sometimes life has a way of laughing at our plans. My lofty thoughts of ordering iced coffee and scones, while building my foundation, came to an abrupt halt when my former employer denied my unemployment benefits. Afraid of the possibility of living under a bridge with a 'Will Work For Food' sign or having to move in with family or friends sent me into a panic. A little dramatic, yes…but accurate. I then began to spend 50-60 hours a week filling out job applications and going on interviews. After two months of searching, I took a job with another top 100 company to work for, but with a twelve thousand dollar pay cut. Taking the position was not the best decision for my overall career, but it kept food on the table and my bills paid. Completely pushing my dreams further into the background of my life, I worked with this company for a few years before leaving for a smaller company that offered me nine thousand dollars more, but no benefits. I jumped at the opportunity to earn more money, but at an expense that I was not fully aware of at the time.

So, there I sat in my car crying and remembering the dreams that I had for myself. I had no one to blame for my current path but myself. I had sold my dreams for a paycheck. Nothing inside of me dared to bring my dreams forward in all of those years of seeking material comfort. Truly, there must have been something inside of me that would have allowed me to multi-task my dreams and work, but I had not even attempted. In that moment of silence in the parking garage, the realization of my decisions were too much for me manage, so I sat there crying for the innocent dreamer in me who had died.

I eventually got out of my car, snuck into the office, and rushed to the restroom to wash my face and pull myself together. However, my thoughts of escape never left me. I decided right then and there that it was time for me to sink or swim. I needed to bet on me for a change of pace. Truth has a way of crashing down on us when we do not expect it. That moring, I learned that working for money instead of working to make a difference in this world was holding me back and was the root of my unhappiness.

November 6, 2012, was a day filled with emotions and results. From watching the Electoral College votes roll in state by state on CNN, to anxiously waiting for the timer in my cousin's kitchen to give me permission to check the results of my home pregnancy test. I was completely on edge. One line meant that life continued along its normal path, but two lines would indicate a change in every aspect of my life. I was afraid of what a positive result would mean, but saddened by the thought of seeing only one line. After seven minutes, four lines, and two positive tests, I knew it was time for me to make some hard decisions about the direction of my life. I no longer had to plan for one, but two.

My child was not planned, but God had a plan. Despite the words of others, I stood on Romans 8:28: "And we know that God causes everything to work together for the good of those who love God and are called according to His purpose for them." I knew I loved God, and I knew He had called me to fulfill His purpose. Once I discovered I was pregnant, I had to shut out the negative people in my life. There were some folks who were bold enough to tell me that I should abort my child because I was teaching teen girls, but I refused to cover one bad decision with another bad decision. I even had to shut down her father because he didn't want me to have her for his own selfish reasons. I accepted the fact that I would have to do this alone. I wasn't sure how I was going to do it, but I knew I could do it and that I had eight months to prepare.

As I prepared for the arrival of my bundle of joy, I made the firm decision to focus on working for myself. I wanted the child that I was carrying to have the best parts of me, and I did not believe sharing me with corporate America was the best decision for my child or myself. I have come to know that being a mom is tough and being an entrepreneur is hard work. Both are extremely rewarding but require long hours, sleepless nights, dedication, and sacrifice. Some days I wish I had more time to spend with my daughter, while at other times, I dream of comforting moments at the spa with long glasses of sweetness.

Daring to be a mompreneur is not for the faint of heart. It mandates an ability to manage multiple projects, personalities, and demands smoothly. As a mompreneur who has chosen to care for her child during the day, several challenges tend to arise. From balancing conference and coaching calls to being attentive to my daughter's immediate needs. There have been countless times when I have had to take my daughter with me to meetings, and sometimes I have been forced to leave meetings early or cancel them all together in order to tend to her needs.

There is a difference between saying we are going to do something and actually doing it. As I sat with life growing inside of me, I knew what I needed to do, but wanted to consult with God on when to move. The first decision I made towards becoming an entrepreneur was to type my letter of resignation and save it to my work computer. I told God that I would wait for him to tell me when to push the send button. I then decided to move back home with my mother. I needed the emotional support and to cut my expenses in half. After these two decisions were made, I began advertising my services in my community by holding free classes at my local library.

I arrived at the library excited about the possibility of sharing my gifts with my community, but as the minutes passed and no one came, I felt defeated. I questioned my sanity and if I was making the right decision. I had made the flyers, snacks, and put on my cutest outfit while pouring my heart and soul into this event. Yet, no one showed up. I expected the room to be overflowing. I knew the goodness of Village of Truth Academy and its potential to become a nationwide program, but the people whom I wanted to serve had not shown their support. I felt like a failure.

As I sat in that empty room feeling sorry for myself and quickly drifting into a pity party, I stopped and thanked God for giving me life, having a place to live, and the love and support of a caring family. I knew God had a plan for me, but in that moment, I was overcome with sadness and even begun to question God.

"God, I am really angry with you right now. I am very bitter. I do not understand why you would bring me to this place just to drop me," I said as a tear escaped my right eye.

Tired and confused, I began packing my things, when I suddenly heard the words of my pastor. The previous Sunday he had preached about being called to a purpose and doing what God calls us to do no matter who is around to witness it. My pastor went on to say that sometimes God just wants to know we will be obedient regardless of what our current situation looks like. He said, "When God tells you to do something, you just do it." Then he said, "If you all do not show up next Sunday, I will preach to the empty pews." This last portion of his sermon would not leave my spirit; it kept replaying in my mind.

I looked around the empty room and told God that I would speak to the empty chairs. I grabbed my syllabus, and with tears in my eyes and a big lump in my throat, I presented my orientation to the empty chairs. I needed this moment to feel as real as possible. As I was finishing, a young lady walking by saw my snacks and decided to come in and inquire. I told her briefly about Village of Truth, Inc., making it sound fun and exciting as I wiped my tears away. I was glad she dropped in and wanted her to stay, but she was unable because her mother was waiting in the car. After a brief pause, she looked at me and told me that she would be right back. I did not believe I would see her again, but when she returned, I was filled with joy.

The following week I was laid off. A part of me was happy because I had asked God to deliver me from my job, but then the reality of being jobless once again hit me like a ton of bricks. I tried to quiet the fear running through me, but it was slowly seeping through as I questioned God's purpose for my life. I could not understand why doors were closing when I was trying to walk in His will, but then again, no one said it would be easy. I knew in my heart things that are easily obtained are rarely valued and that God was sending me through a time of polishing and preparation. So, I decided to trust the journey that God was creating for me. That decision motivated and excited me to move forward with my dreams.

What I've learned is that everyone is not destined to the same thing and we all have a different road to travel in life. During my start-up, friends and family would often mock my belief that God had called me to start Village of Truth, Inc. Some would go as far as to say, "You're saying God called you to be poor?" My favorite was, "So God told you to live off of your momma?" I often listened in silence because I could not defend what God had told me to do because it was for me.

One of my mentors spoke life over me when she said, "Your comfort zone is where your dreams go to die." For when we are comfortable, we do not allow for growth, renewal, or transformation. I needed those words because I was so uncomfortable at the time, but I was where I was supposed to be. From speaking to the empty chairs at the library to my first class of girls completing the program, God was guiding my steps. My first set of young ladies trusted me and valued my opinions. They allowed me to work out all the kinks of my program, from booking engaging speakers to diversifying the learning tools that I utilized.

Less than two weeks after my first group ended, I received an opportunity to present my program to a local group home with eighteen girls. They didn't have a budget, so I did it for free. A few months later, they asked me to come back and offered me a small stipend that covered my gas for the week. This time, however, I was able to meet several other group home administrators. In addition, I was given the opportunity to present my foundations program at a local high school for two semesters. Unfortunately, they did not have a budget, but a larger audience. I was excited by the opportunities that were presenting themselves; however, I needed compensation for my work.

Just as I was ready to reevaluate my decision to be an entrepreneur, God placed a wonderful woman in my path from the high school where I mentored students. Over the course of the next year, I was contracted to teach life skills in four high schools in Los Angeles County as well as another foundation. All of the job openings paid very well. I went from having four students meeting in the library to 190 students a week. What seemed like a mist from a sprinkler turned into a trickle of rain and then into a flood of blessings. By the grace of God, it became a tsunami of His promises.

As a mother, I have had to make difficult decisions. There are no shortcuts to success. You have to be willing to be uncomfortable.

During the last few years, I have learned that faith (believing God will do it) and trust (letting God do it in His own time) are inseparable. There were days when I felt God had left me alone, and there were times when I knew His grace and mercy had opened the door.

Resilient women know the same God who holds up the sun and holds back the sea surely will carry them when they are unable to walk alone. Strong women bet it all on themselves. They relentlessly pursue their purpose by willing doors to open. I learned you cannot put fifty percent of your poker chips on building corporate America and fifty percent on building your company and beat the odds. You have to find a way to elevate your dreams first. In this life, you must learn to bet on YOU, because successful women are not made to break even. We break out!

My successful secret is to be resilient. We have all had to be tough or bounce back from something in life. The goal is to feel the pain and then let it drive you instead of letting it kill you. Resilience comes with faith and with the revelation that God will sustain you through it all. Even when you think you have hit rock bottom, know that you have the power to move forward and survive because you are strong, ready, and willing to do what it takes to become the person you always wanted to be.

*"Character cannot be developed in ease and quiet. Only through experience of trial and suffering can the soul be strengthened, ambition inspired, and success achieved."*

~ Helen Keller

# Chapter 15

# BRAND YOUR LIFE

## Juanita Aguerrebere

My journey as an entrepreneur started ten years ago. It was a sunny day filled with a thick humidity at the lagoon. I was there for the Hawaii State Canoe Paddling Regatta. Even though I had competed at States before, my current situation did not leave time for paddling with my canoe club. I was visiting my friends to cheer them on, but inside, I felt crushed and overwhelmed. I was a single mom, recently divorced, and found myself juggling two jobs as an archaeologist and waitress. The reality had set in that my career as an archaeologist, a dream I had since I was a child, was just a job and I was broke. I had gone from living in an exclusive neighborhood with a lifestyle of world travel, elite country clubs, and shopping at Neiman Marcus to a one-room studio and drowning in compounding debt. I moved to Hawaii when I was nineteen and was now a single mom feeling all alone. I felt stuck on this rock, not wanting to leave my daughter Samantha and not wanting to stay.

Things are much different. One morning, I was swimming in the ocean as the crisp, cool water invigorated my body and spirit. As I dove down among coral heads and fish, a feeling of bliss started to settle in. I swam back up and then floated on my back while staring at the blue sky filled with white clouds. I felt blessed to be living in Hawaii. The feeling of bliss percolated through my head and down until I felt a sense of gratitude emanating throughout my body. When the sensation hit my feet, I started to wiggle my toes and a smile overwhelmed my face. As I swam back to shore, I let the energy of the waves do the work; it felt as if I was expending no energy myself. I walked back to my car, sat in the driver's seat, and was surprised to find my body shaking like I had just done a heavy cardio workout. I felt quite energized, joyful, and excited. My soul sent out a vibration of peace, love, and happiness. I am amazed at the life I have created and how far I have come on this road as an entrepreneur.

I am a mother to four beautiful children, and I have a loving partner, Isaac, who supports and challenges me in my growth. He is the father of my three boys, Blaise, Antonio Joaquin, and "Pancho". I own a web and social media consulting company in addition to being a co-owner with my partner of Aquahunters, a kayak fishing sports league. We now live in the home that I always wanted, and my businesses are taking off. As a mompreneur, I played a key role as a founding boardmember during the startup phase of a private school that my kids currently attend. I now have complete liberty in my life. I get to decide what I do each day, and I truly appreciate how far I have come on this journey as an entrepreneur - the lows and highs. Yet, even on my darkest days, my fierce determination with being a mompreneur and making a positive difference in the world has always been my navigational guide.

My journey as an entrepreneur started the day I met Isaac. As I walked across the regatta, I had no idea how this tall, dark, and handsome Hawaiian paddler waving at me would impact my life. I was fortunate to run into him again by chance at Aloha Tower where hundreds of the state's top paddlers were celebrating. It was the weekend, and I had thirty dollars left in my account, with payday a whole six days away. But, with some encouragement from my friends, I found myself driving to the party solo.

As I was walking to the entrance of Aloha Tower, I saw him standing there by himself against a pillar. This time, I found myself being drawn to him, but I kept on walking to look for an ATM. I needed cash to buy my ticket for the party. When I heard heavy footsteps behind me, I turned around to ask for directions. There he was with his arm extended and index finger pointed as if he were about to tap me on the shoulder. His face was frozen in shock that I had turned around so suddenly. He stopped and turned to go in the opposite direction. Laughing, I asked him for directions to the ATM. He pointed to it, and I noticed I had walked right past it. I must have been daydreaming to have missed it in the first place. He then explained to me that he was about to introduce himself but chickened out. *Obviously,* I thought. Then he asked, "Weren't you the girl in the green skirt that I saw before?" Isaac had caught my attention and never lost it.

At the party, we were able to have a down-to-earth conversation about what he felt his purpose was in life. Isaac told me that what he loved to do more than anything was fish off of a kayak. How interesting was that? At first, I laughed hysterically because there we were amongst the state's elite canoe paddlers and he was talking about fishing off of a *plastic* kayak that tourists use to paddle. I was curious to find out how he could think kayak fishing was better than canoe paddling. After all, he was a state champion like myself. After listening to his adventures, I prompted him to consider doing it as a business.

"What do you mean? Nobody does this. How could I possibly make a living doing this?" Isaac asked me.

I then went into brainstorming mode of all the ways he could do it as a living. I compared the billion-dollar industry of surfing, its ecosystem of businesses within the sport as a model for kayak fishing. Isaac reminded me that there was one problem; nobody was doing it. I told him that as a Native Hawaiian, his ancestors did this in an accent form. Thousands of people before Isaac had done this as a way of life, so why couldn't he? All of a sudden, I saw Duke Kahanamoku flash before my eyes. He is known as the father of surfing and for introducing the Native Hawaiian sport to the world.

"You could be the father of kayak fishing," I told Isaac. "It's going to be your job to spread it to the world!"

I had been dating Isaac for about six months, when my daughter and I flew to my parent's home in Washington, D.C. for Christmas. While I was visiting, my dad gave me a book that changed my life. It was called *Rich Dad Poor Dad*. From the moment I started reading it, I knew I was always meant to be an entrepreneur. I had found my "kind".

Isaac and I began taking business classes together. We knew we wanted to be entrepreneurs, and I was excited about Isaac's dream. I quit my part-time job so I could totally concentrate on becoming educated on business. I was convinced a good business would be the ticket to creating the life of our dreams. I read hundreds of books and wanted to give myself an education equivalent to an MBA without going back to school. Isaac was very enouraging and believed I could figure out a way to work from home. Honestly, I wasn't too convinced, but Isaac believed in me the way I believed in him.

I was still an archaeologist either in the field or traveling, not an ideal situation for a single mom. At the time, I really desired to be a web developer and a computer genius, but the story in my head told me that was not for women. Instead, I focused my energy on working with Isaac, and we mapped out his vision for the sport of kayak fishing. We figured out a game plan and wrote a ten-, twenty-, and thirty-year vision for Aquahunters, a kayak fishing sports league. We knew that in order to look big and hit the world, we needed a great looking website.

When Isaac received a quote of five thousand dollars for the creation of a website, I decided to rebirth my dream of web developing and figure it out. After my first client, I was ready to take on the world with my new business. I fell in love with the field of website development. The learning curve was high, and I was hungry to learn as much as I could. I truly felt I was at the right place at the right time. From there on, my work became a word-of-mouth referral business. Thank goodness I figured it out just in time for the birth of our son.

Being a business owner is an American dream, and we found the startup phase to be filled with challenges. As I started getting new clients, we found ourselves facing eviction despite Isaac's forty-hour plus workweek. We were investing our own money into Aquahunters; kayaks and fishing gear was expensive. We needed to get a handle on our cash flow. We sacrificed every non-essential to keep Aquahunters going, including having a television. This sacrifice allowed us to focus our energy on our business and eliminating it allowed us to have more time; we vowed to never bring it in our home again. Unfortunately, this was not enough, and we were evicted when I was seven months pregnant with our second son.

I challenged myself to create a tech venture when we moved in with a friend of ours who allowed use to stay in her guest bedroom. I was given an iPhone as a gift, and I realized that having a smartphone could create mobile solutions for the everyday person. This inspired me to create the first iPhone business directory for Hawaii that I named after my son Blaise. I started selling my directory to local businesses, and soon, I was making enough money to help us get back on our feet. I set a ninety-day goal to find a home that would fit within our budget and was within two blocks of the beach. Three months later, we moved into a two-bedroom cottage one block from the beach. I gave birth a week later.

Wanting to do more, I entered my tech venture in the Hawaii Entrepreneur Investor Pitch Competition. After an extensive application process and three rounds, I was chosen as a finalist. I had the opportunity to pitch my venture to a panelist of judges for the big event and was told by the judges that they did not think people in Hawaii would be searching for local places on their phones. Therefore, I didn't win. Crushed by the news, I slowly stopped my venture. Looking back, I actually had an idea that was ahead of its time. Now I can find people on their iPhones everywhere I go in Hawaii. This became a powerful lesson where I learned to continuously ask myself, "Who do I believe and who do I listen to?" It served as a reminder to trust and believe in myself at all times.

Running a household, two businesses, and raising four amazing kids plus a dog can be a juggling act. At times, I feel like I'm a crazy magician about to lose my mind, knowing that at any moment a child could get sick, a project may fall through, a deadline may be missed, and a school lunch left in the car. However, I pray a lot, and that's what helps to get me by. I also plan ahead and then go into action by implementing a system to create solutions for any problem that crosses my path. When many woman are faced with a problem, they don't look for the solution. As a mompreneur, we find solutions.

The self-perceived failure of my tech venture created a jump in my evolution as a mompreneur, and I was on fire. I began creating a network of supportive entrepreneurs, mentors, and coaches. I became an expert developer and embraced social media into my services. Even though I was doing all of the tech work for my clients, I found I was creating their brand and image, as well. I did not realize how powerful I was at branding until my life was turned upside down by a shark battle.

In April of 2013, Isaac captured footage of him fighting a fish on his line while a shark was battling him for it. When he told me that he thought he captured great footage on his GoPro, I went into strategic planning mode. We were able to have Yahoo break the story, and within a few hours, we had ABC, NBC, FOX, ESPN, and CNN calling. Every news and media company around the world was covering Isaac's story and YouTube video. We attained nine million views in three days and made the homepage of YouTube. The whole world was finding out about Isaac of Aquahunters and the sport of kayak fishing. Our hard work was finally paying off and brought us many opportunities, including filming a reality TV show in our home for two weeks with a Hollywood production company.

The greatest gift for me as a mompreneur is to work from home and set my schedule. The flexibility that I allow myself would not be possible working a nine-to-five. I strive to plan my workday and schedule around my children, and this method works perfect for me. Even during my pregnancies, I would take new clients and make sure the projects were wrapped up before the birth of my child. When my baby was born, I gave myself a cushion of time to recover before going back to work. My newborn babies would sleep a lot and my hormones kept me awake at night, so I utilized that time to take on more projects to accommodate my nocturnal body clock. Many times, I worked at the computer while feeding my baby.

It's essential as a mompreneur to create systems that flow with your family and business. The key is to create a system around caring for your family and business to see what works. Implement your system until it becomes a routine and revise it as your family grows. It is important to set boundaries and rules that work for you. I will share three golden rules that work for me and for others that I have shared them with.

First, I always keep my calendar open and only commit to essential meetings or events. This applies to both my business and family, which means I say no more often than yes. It's okay to say no if you cannot commit one hundred percent. The result is that I do not overcommit myself, because I believe in creating quality experiences for my clients. Second, I treat being a mother the same as if I was a professional athlete. I take time to eat, stay fit, and rest like an athlete. The result is that I stay healthier and so does my family. Last but not least, I set the example for my children when interacting with other people so they can model this same behavior. The result is happy, well-behaved kids.

Sometimes I feel as though all odds are against me, and at the same time, I feel as though I was divinely chosen to be of service to this world. I can tell you that both serves me, but I didn't realize that in the beginning of my journey. It wasn't until I received assistance from coaches and mentors who had "walked the talk" that I was able to understand myself and share my story. Once I was willing to embrace myself, my life as a mompreneur became much easier. I then created my own personal brand and was able to share my authentic self with the world and attract my dream clients. I am a branding expert who enjoys making my clients rich or famous through social media. This was something not available years ago, but as we enter further into the digital age, our lives are becoming more transparent. Embrace technology and leverage it to share the story of you. Brands that consistently share an authentic and engaging story will win the game of business. Treat yourself as a personal brand and be authentic with your customers. Use social media as a two-way conversation instead of free advertisement. When you make mistakes, acknowledge them, learn from them, and move on.

Leveraging our access to technology is what allows us to compete with top businesses and organizations across the world. It is my belief that mothers are rightful leaders, and together we have life experiences to run the most successful business or organization on the planet. So, I ask you, what are you willing to share with the world? What difference would you make if your story went viral? I want you to know that I am your biggest cheerleader on this journey of being a mompreneur. I am rooting for you. I know you CAN do this!

My successful secret is to brand all facets of your life into your business. When your business reflects your lifestyle and your authentic self, you will attract the ideal clients that you want to show up. Be sure to brand yourself on a daily basis. When I talk about branding, it's about getting more exposure every day until the world knows your name. Soon, you will have built a loyal following. Ever heard the saying, build it and they will come? Well, it's true! I implore you to try it because it works, and one of the fastest ways to leverage yourself is by making connections with people on social media. You always want to look for future collaborators, friends, and mentors. Also, share and support others on a massive scale and great things will come back to you bigger and better.

*"A strong, positive self-image is the best possible preparation for success."*
~ Joyce Brothers

# Chapter 16

## WRITING MY OWN LEGACY

### Tiffany Bethea

I have a vision of my great-grandchildren. I see them walking up to my picture hanging in their home and kissing it; not just because they love me and miss me, but because they appreciate the choices I made and how their lives have been impacted because of those choices. I see this image in my head regularly and often unprompted. Although I can't picture the face of my offspring who haven't been born yet or the house they will live in, it motivates me and gives me comfort along with strength when I need it. What will be the significance of your name one hundred years from now? What will be your legacy? Have you ever really thought about it? Who's writing the story that will be told of you? I grabbed my pen at the age of twenty-eight and decided to write the story that I want to be told of me long after I'm gone. I decided to change the game and redirect the course for my family.

I should probably tell you that I am a second-generation entrepreneur. Being my own boss is not a new concept to me; it was something I saw modeled at home. I didn't even realize until a few years into being a mompreneur that I was living out what I saw demonstrated by my mother, who is still to this day her own boss. For most of my life, I remember my mother doing what she loved and getting paid for it. As a young child, she was a part-time entrepreneur in addition to working a full-time career that she loved. During my teenage years, she transitioned into her life's assignment and became her own boss for several organizations. Over the years, as she and my dad built businesses, we watched our lives slowly transform because of their courageous decisions. Not only did our zip code change, but our way of life as we knew it elevated.

I'm not sure if it was from watching my mother all those years or if it was something innate, but I always knew I wanted to work for myself. I always pictured myself making my own schedule, serving the world the way I wanted to, traveling, and living a fabulous life. There were several moments, though, where I thought this might not happen. At the time I started my first business, I was also going through a divorce and becoming a single mom. My precious son was still a baby. He would never remember his dad and I being married. My marriage had been such a rollercoaster, and although I was happy to be divorcing, the ride was far from over. My spirit was fatigued; my mind was traumatized; my emotions were numb; my finances were on life support; and my will to live was hanging in the balance.

My divorce reactivated a struggle with depression that I had experienced in my early twenties. Day after day, I struggled to put the pieces of my life back together. The pain and hopelessness sometimes felt as if they were choking me and I would never breathe again. I thought my marriage would last forever. How could this be? My parents were and still are married. How could I be a single mom? What did this mean for my dreams?

I was forced to confront attitudes I didn't realize I had towards single moms and deal with the fact that I was rewriting the plan and starting over. Months of unanswered questions and surmounting pain turned a trying struggle with depression into a raging battle with suicide. Some days, just lifting my head off the pillow took everything in me. There were moments I would just gaze at my baby son's precious face. I felt so inadequate in my pain and brokenness to be the mother he needed me to be. I would toggle back and forth between believing I needed to stay alive for him and thinking he might be better off without me. But, it was learning the power of my will and speaking it over my life that brought me back from the brink. Many days, I walked over to the mirror with a tear-soaked face and said, "YOU WILL LIVE! GET UP! DON'T DIE HERE! THERE IS TOO MUCH LIFE LEFT INSIDE OF YOU! IT'S NOT JUST ABOUT YOU! GO ON! LIVE!"

Ending my marriage caused me to lose two homes, a car, and so much more. Once I fully came to terms with the fact that I was completely starting over, I decided to aim for the sky and go for the gusto. If I had to start over, wouldn't it be a great time to take a stab at making my dreams come true? After all, I had absolutely nothing to lose and everything to gain.

At the age of twenty-eight, I decided enough was enough. I was finished building and supporting everyone else's dreams; it was time to build mine. Utilizing all my years of marketing experience, I decided to become a consultant. I had received my degree in marketing and actually worked for my mom building several of her companies. Because of their non-profit nature, I found myself having to be the entire marketing department with very limited support staff. This afforded me the opportunity to hone several skills, including direct mail campaign coordination, radio and television promotion, graphic design, e-marketing, creative copywriting, and website design and maintenance. Feeling armed with education and experience, I made my plan and took the leap from full-time employee to full-time entrepreneur.

At the beginning of working for myself, I was definitely experiencing the honeymoon period. I loved creating my days and adjusting to not being bound by the hands on the clock. Many people in my sphere of influence were very familiar with my work, so word-of-mouth marketing was my biggest source used to gain clientele. It was wonderful, but after a while, I looked up and realized I had a plan that wasn't detailed enough. What did I really want to accomplish? How did I really envision my business? I had stepped out on my passion of helping people create marketing strategies and amplify their messages to the world. However, a lot of people were familiar with my graphic and web design skills, and somehow, I got stuck in the box. One day, I looked up and said to myself, *How did I become the graphic design lady? This is not what I set out to do.* That's when I realized the vulnerability of new entrepreneurship. I was so pressed to make sure I earned enough income to cover my bills that I didn't always consider if the work was congruent with my plan.

After about the first six months in business, I began struggling. Struggling financially, struggling with my identity, struggling mentally. Had I made a mistake? Maybe I shouldn't have made such a bold move. I was still rebuilding myself personally. Did I have the energy needed to allow my business to flourish while still being a mommy to a young son?

I also struggled with time management. The demands of growing a consulting business were overwhelming. Many times my son would need me, and in the back of my mind I would be thinking, "I need me right now." I would cook dinner while at the same time talking to potential clients. Anytime my business phone rang, I felt like a slave to it; the lines of business and personal became blurred. This was not how I had imagined my entrepreneurial life. I had no social life. I was always either mommy or marketing consultant. Everyone got what they needed from me, except me. I was tired, burned out, and lost. Even though my ex-husband was consistently spending time with our son, oftentimes I was completely exhausted and couldn't move by the time my break came.

In my starvation for business, I continued to attract the wrong clients. I found myself working with people who were draining the life out of me with their unrealistic expectations that I felt obligated to accommodate. I also struggled with pricing structure. I was charging pennies compared to what I was worth. Completing thousands of dollars' worth of work for pennies on the dollar has a way of totally demotivating you. I knew what I should have been charging, but I just didn't have the courage to demand it. So, month in and month out, my revenue fell enormously short of what it should and could have been. I was barely getting by, at the end of my rope, and ready to give up.

Finally, I got the break I was waiting for! I had a meeting with a potential client. They weren't ready to begin work just yet, but someone who had been present during the consultation was so impressed that they called a friend of the family who was the president of another corporation. This company, who was also in need of marketing services, called me shortly after my consultation meeting. Happy to hear from them, I quickly put together a proposal. After continuing to nurture the possibility, we finally got to the place of contract signing. Oh happy day! By now, I was ready to charge what I was worth. I will never forget discussing my consulting fee with them. When they agreed, I almost fell out of my chair. It was my biggest payday yet. I had landed a huge contract. I was so excited; all of the pain and frustration up to that point had been worth it. I had a bonafide contract doing what I initially set out to do. It was wonderful.

I loved life! Money was flowing in consistently; I owned my time; and I was finding balance and true healing. Then it all came to a sudden stop. I received a strange email from the president of the company that stated there was an urgent matter and they were trying to reach me. When we finally connected, we had a conversation I wished we had not. They were going bankrupt and needed to stop services immediately. Despite it being a breach of contract, I would learn there was really nothing I could do. If I had taken them to court and won, there were no assets to collect on. They were completely broke. How could this be? It felt like the rug had been pulled from under me. The contract was my biggest payday and my struggle had just ended. Now I would have very little time to bounce back. I had other smaller paid projects, but this was my main monthly retainer client that truly allowed me to pay my bills. I was honestly devastated and started to wonder if entrepreneurship just wasn't for me.

Back to the struggle I went. Still, it was a defining moment. In this rebuilding space, I had the "aha" moment that would change the course of my business forever. I was determined not to fail, but I realized I needed some help. I couldn't do it alone; I needed to follow someone who was already doing it successfully. I soon started praying for a mentor or coach who could reveal what I was missing. It wouldn't be long before I found just that. Working with my mentor, I began to get to the root of how I was called to serve the world. I pulled my website down and put up a temporary one for six months while I took my time and questioned everything. When I relaunched, I wanted it to be right. I looked in depth at my services, my systems, and everything taking place in my business. Most importantly, I took a look in the mirror and got real about who was leading the business. I invested more time in personal development than business development; as I got more life clarity, I got more business clarity.

Finally, the time came when I was ready to relaunch my business! After the downtime, I was spiritually refreshed, emotionally energized, financially stable, and mentally fortified. I was ready! I relaunched my website, revised my plan, and totally rebranded. It was amazing! Business started flowing in left and right, not just any business but quality business. I started attracting dream projects and working within my niche. Before long, I looked up to find myself actually doing what I had set out to do, and I was absolutely loving it. I was happier, a better mom, and an all around better me.

Are you ready to write your own legacy? The biggest thing I learned that turned my business around is that personal development is a catalyst for business development. Say to yourself, "I AM MY BUSINESS!" Your business will not outgrow you. But, as you continue to develop and improve, it will spark the same in your business.

ASSESS YOUR RESOURCES! One of the biggest struggles I had to overcome was working outside of the reality of the resources I had. I was in denial, but when I confronted this headon, it was a powerful turning point in my business. The time resource was the one I had to get real about. Being the single mom of a young son, I had to be honest about the fact that I didn't have as much time as my single childless friends in business. I would be so frustrated because I couldn't seem to get anything done, and I was always exhausted. Then I became committed to the idea of living by a block week schedule. This allowed me to structure my time and make myself accountable for when I was to wear which hat. I had been guilty of being marketing consultant at times when I really should have just been mommy. Don't beat yourself up if you do this; we have all been there. Structuring your time allows you to be one hundred percent present wherever you are. Now when I am in mommy mode, I am just mommy. I'm not worried about my clients or anything else, just enjoying my little prince.

The clarity and focus I have when it is time to be marketing consultant is strengthened now because the lines are no longer blurred. Assess your time, money, skill, and all of your resources. Get real about what you are working with. No matter what the starting point, YOU CAN GET THERE! No matter how much time, money, etc. you have or don't have, don't let that stop you. Get real about what you are working with! Once you assess the resources you are actually working with, put together a plan that allows you to do what's necessary for your business with those resources until you have new ones. I don't have as much time as I would like, but for now, I work the time I have and am working it!

MARK YOUR MOTIVATION! My son is my biggest source of motivation, not only him but also the generations following him. I am charting a course now that will enable them to have a better life than I could ever dream of. Each generation will succeed the previous generation. This is one of my most driving factors. I am writing a legacy of purpose, fulfillment, and of financial and time freedom. So, even on days where I am overwhelmed by juggling the demands of mommyhood with the demands of the two businesses I now have, I envision my great-grandchildren kissing that picture of me on the wall. I am determined not to let my current struggles and challenges cause them to experience the same challenges. I will push through my challenges now so they never have to face the same ones.

What is holding you back? What is keeping you from moving forward to the next place? If your children and their children and their children were standing in front of you with the question of why their lives aren't better, will your current excuses hold up? Wll you be able to look them in the face and tell them what's holding you back right now is the reason why they are facing the same challenges? If not, then use this as motivation to get going or keep going!

RECLAIM THE PEN and write your own legacy! Entrepreneurship

is about so much more than money. Seeing how my parents' choices transformed my life, I feel the same obligation to take the torch and continue running. Whose life is impacted by your courage to take action? How will the story be told generations from now? Nothing that is currently in your way can stop you! And if the circumstances of life have caused you to struggle with depression or possibly have suicidal thoughts, then I tell you, too, YOU WILL LIVE! GET UP! DON'T DIE HERE! THERE IS TOO MUCH LIFE LEFT INSIDE OF YOU! IT'S NOT JUST ABOUT YOU! GO ON! LIVE! Live your story out loud. Let it be told boldly. We need you! We need you to thrive!

My successful secret is to get clear on who your beneficiaries are. Your life is part of a larger master plan. All you do and experience is so much greater than just you. Our God plans for generations and we should, also. There are those coming behind us who are in need of us fulfilling our assignment so they can find and fulfill theirs. I'm not sure what my life would be like without my parents demonstrating success and entrepreneurship in front of me. I'm sure I could have still located my assignment, but I believe it would have been a more difficult search. Are you clear on whose life is directly affected by the path you are trailblazing right now? Determine that they won't have the same starting point as you, and allow this determination to motivate you to clear the path for them now.

*"Success is the sum of small efforts — repeated day in and day out."*

~ Robert Collier

# PLAY TIME IS OVER

## Cheryl Wood

I must admit that I find mompreneurs to be some of the most talented women in the world. After all, not only do we manage successful enterprises, oftentimes as a one-woman-show (especially in the first five years of business), but we also manage the daily needs of our children who rely on us for every aspect of the word "mom". Before we ever serve our clients, we first serve our households as maids, nurses, chefs, chauffers, butlers, teachers, and guidance counselors without ever receiving a paycheck, vacation day, or sick leave. Yet, somehow, we find a way to balance it all and do it with a smile!

Ironically, as I provide business coaching to passionate mompreneurs across the country, I have come to realize that many mompreneurs have passion and drive for their business but are keeping themselves stagnate from achieving the level of success they truly desire. Most often, the problem is not a lack of talent or expertise that prevents success, but rather personal fears and self-limiting beliefs about what is possible. Oftentimes, it is the fear of expanding their thinking, taking risks, and playing bigger that keeps mompreneurs stagnate.

But, here's the reality: the longer you hold yourself hostage to fear and what is comfortable, the longer you are robbing yourself of the opportunity to create success on your own terms, to experience time freedom (the one thing every mompreneur craves), to create a legacy, and to build generational wealth. So, starting now, as you are reading this book, acknowledge four powerful words that you will allow to guide your entrepreneurial journey: Play Time Is Over!

Play Time Is Over is a powerful self-affirmation that signifies you will not waste another minute focused on what you are fearful of or staying in a zone of comfort that is not conducive to growth. Rather, you will become intentional about achieving your dreams by moving beyond your realm of comfort, taking risks, and embracing your fears.

As a mom of three – now ages 6, 7, and 10 – I often reflect on the way things were in my life just five years ago, and sometimes, I barely recognize my own life. Five years ago, I was a frustrated mom frantically running the corporate rat race and holding myself hostage to that reality. I had convinced myself that I could never be "one of those people" who actually lived their dreams. I spoke life to the things I didn't want instead of the things I did want. I wasted time wallowing in all the reasons why I couldn't have more, couldn't create a different life, couldn't experience abundance and prosperity, couldn't develop a different future, couldn't walk in my destiny, and couldn't pursue my passion. I assumed creating a life void of punching a timeclock and building someone else's dream was a bunch of FLUFF!

I had a scarcity mindset and thought I had to have everything perfectly aligned to become successful – the right resources, education, finances, network, and connections. But, one day, I decided to do something different. I decided to take a chance on myself and give fear a kick in the gut. Over time, I began to discover that my ability to be great was nothing more than my willingness to abandon comfort in order to intentionally nurture my possibilities. I learned to identify the things that bring me the most fear and to run towards those things instead of running away from them. Why? Because greatness only manifests itself on the other side of fear.

The great news is that you have the same opportunity. Greatness is waiting for you to show up, not the other way around. As a mompreneur, start to expand your expectations and stretch your thinking. Acknowledge that comfort is overrated! Do not keep yourself from a life of joy, passion, fulfillment, service, abundance, and prosperity because of fear of the unknown. Instead, get comfortable with discomfort.

In my personal experience, I find there are three success strategies that support mompreneurs in moving closer to success as they commit to the Play Time Is Over motto.

The first success strategy is to upgrade your internal dialogue. It is a common tendency for mompreneurs to discount their own talent and abilities, but here is where a shift is mandatory. You must become your own biggest cheerleader. Whenever you hear negative self-chatter starting to brew internally, combat it with positive, empowering self-talk and ask these potent questions: *Why not me? Why not now?* There is no magic formula for achieving success, so if anyone is going to achieve it, why not you and why not now?

The second success strategy is to develop focus. Focus encompasses four parts: (1) Focus on what you want and stay in your lane; drown out external noise and distractions, (2) focus on executing one idea at a time; avoid "idea overwhelm" and becoming consumed with too many ideas at once, (3) focus more on what you have than what you are lacking; don't allow a negative focus on what you don't have to stifle your movement, and (4) focus on "why" not "how"; you won't always know "how" your big dream and your business success is going to manifest, but your "why" will help you to keep your eyes on the prize without a thought of throwing in the towel.

The third success strategy is to find some iron. You've undoubtedly heard the expression "iron sharpens iron". So, seek out other passionate, mission-driven mompreneurs who have the same drive, conviction, and determination that you do for living their dreams and growing successful, profitable businesses. Create your own "community of dream builders" who support you, uplift you, energize you, share ideas and resources, and hold you accountable. It is impossible to succeed in business as an island all to yourself. Community is vital, but you have a say in who's in the community!

As you implement these success strategies, remember that your journey to entrepreneurial success is not supposed to be easy or else everyone would be doing it. Commit to the time, work, effort, and sacrifices that are required, and avoid falling into the trap of being a Professional Procrastinator, a Wimpy Whiner, a Picky Perfectionist, or an Elaborate Excuse-Maker. Simply be an ACTION-TAKER who keeps executing until you achieve the success you want.

Continue on your course as an empowered mompreneur working to live your dream. Never diminish your gifts or dim your light. Your story, your experiences, your talents, and your gifts are necessary in the world! Remember, greatness is waiting for you to show up, not the other way around.

Don't ever stop moving forward, because "while you're making excuses, somebody else will be executing."

Play Time Is Over!

# Conclusion

# PATRICE TARTT

## Chief Mommy Diva

It is Wednesday and the last week of school, and I have completed all three of my final assignments that are due by Friday. Normally, I try to stay on top of my homework, because after school, I like being in the mix of the ladies stopping in to the salon for a visit to get "beautified". It's something about looking up to women who know the exact meaning of self-care and stepping away from their kids, even if it is only for a few hours. Every woman, especially moms, deserve to be pampered. It's rejuviating, relaxing, and refreshing. As for me, life is not so stressful when you don't have bills to pay, and I won't have to do that until I graduate from college. So, it will be easy living until I am older and out on my own.

I actually like watching these women get a variety of services from manicures, pedicures, paraffin treatments, or just a new haircut or style. Most of the time, this place is pretty busy. The owner is simply phenomenal. I truly admire her, and I definitely plan to be just like her when I grow up. She is resilient, a go-getter, a hustler, a nail technician, a mompreneur, and the Queen Mommy Diva. She is my mother!

When I think back to when I was in grade school, the spring of '96 to be more specific, I was in the fifth grade. This is when I gained my initial exposure to mompreneurship. My mother left corporate America and started a nail salon called Tip Top Nails. She also had a station for a licensed cosmetologist. Not only did she start a business, but she *successfully* ran her business.

A couple of things that made her different from all the other nail salons in the area was that she was well versed with the latest in her field as a licensed nail technician, and she welcomed men to services that mostly only women received during that time. She had a sign that read "Men Welcome" and went as far as creating manicures and pedicures customized for men, such as the sports manicure and pedicure. She built her clientele quickly because of the stellar service that she provided. Her clients were regulars and knew that every time they visited my mother's salon, they were going to receive "tip-top quality service" in a comfortable and relaxing environment.

Back in the '90s, nail salons were opening up on every block. However, she was one of only a few African-Americans to operate a nail salon in Milwaukee, Wisconsin. Her passion was ensuring her clients were satisfied by providing service they could not receive anywhere else. If a pedicure took only forty minutes at one salon, her pedicure would take an hour and twenty minutes.

She truly enjoyed the flexibility and freedom of working for herself and being able to spend more time with her daughter, me. I loved it because not only did she have more time to spend with me, but I would get the best manicures and pedicures in town! It became a win-win for us. During the '90s, there was no such thing as social media presence or even social media for that matter. So, you had one of two choices: sink or swim. And my mother swam! She had the competitive edge that many of her local competitiors simply did not have. My mother built a brand that no one could duplicate at that time. Her competitive edge was always being on time, flexible with her schedule, providing quality service, offering a variety of services customized for men and women, consistency, and extra time with her clients so they never felt rushed.

As I reflect back, it is simply memories, and memories are what help to build the foundation for us to better ourselves. We are always thinking back on the past, whether it's good, bad, or indifferent. When we do this, it is healthy. Memories assist us in knowing what works and what doesn't work, and the past can help to make us better at what we do. Having a "lessons learned box" nearby never hurts either. I say all of this to say that in both life and business, sometimes we need to be able to do a self-assessment to make sure that our passion is aligned properly with our destiny. At a young age, I had a great coach and mentor, my mother, so my memories on mompreneurship are great and this is what has helped to make me the mompreneur that I am today. Remembering the example my mother set when I was child along with the lessons that she taught on the fundamentals of running a successful business is why I am successful. To the Queen Mommy Diva on the Move, I SALUTE and thank you!

By now you know that as moms and entrepreneurs, we are each a superwoman in our own right. Life will never be perfect, however living a harmonious lifestyle makes things a whole lot easier. You now understand how all sixteen of us have overcome obstacles, combated challenges and triumped over tragedy. I never said that the road to mompreneurship was going to be easy, but it is attainable. I watched my mother when I was a kid do the exact same thing that all of us have done, she started a business and was successful. I don't call her the Queen Mommy Diva for nothing! She is the epitome of those three words.

I truly hope that each of you take something away from this book as we have all poured out our knowledge and secrets to success, and I look forward to hearing from you on how *Mommy Divas on the Move: 16 Successful Secrets for Mompreneurs* has inspired, motivated and helped you to walk your journey driven by your passion to your destiny.

# NICOLE ROBERTS JONES

## The "Bonus Mommy" Diva on the Move

When I heard of Patrice's work in pulling together sixteen mompreneurs to tell their stories, I was ecstatic when she asked me to be a part of it. You see, many of the women I have coached over the last twenty years—although they may be single, married, divorced, and widowed entrepreneurs or corporate executives—have one thing in common; they are mothers. Mothers who move and have their being in their own calling, while actively holding the space to love and nurture their children as they grow. This is a true juggling act.

For a mompreneur, the notion of having to balance it all is an everyday reality of synchronizing work and home but finding time for herself, as well. Every one of my Mommy Diva coaching clients struggle with being the best possible parent to their child(ren), the best possible mate to her partner, and girlfriend to her sista friends on top of trying to keep her image, mindset, body, and health intact. Yes, every mommy I work with strives to have it all!

In this struggle toward having it all, she often feels guilty or like a failure when one of those many balls she's juggling drops. Without a system in place that supports them having it all, this struggle can take its toll. This is why I love working with mommies as a coach; so I can help them create the harmony needed in their business and personal lives in order for them to live the life they love and love the life they live! While I have worked with many mompreneur clients in creating that harmony, it's a struggle that is very personal for me, as well.

When I met my husband in 2004, I instantly became what I call a "bonus mommy". For those of you who are wondering what is a bonus mommy, most folks would call this a stepmother, but I don't use the word "step" as I think that word is so harsh. I know that the role I play in the lives of my husband's children is a bonus…an added blessing. I am clear that my bonus kids have a mom, and I am not here to replace her. However, what I have gotten from them being in my life and me being in theirs is a bonus…a gift to my life. There is an African adage that says, "It takes a village to raise a child", and as a bonus mommy, I become a part of that village.

As a bonus mommy, I work in concert with my children's mother to add harmony, love, and support. This is a balancing act in and of itself, so in addition to me having to balance all the things of a typical mother, I am also balancing two lives that blend into one – my life with my husband and our lives with my bonus children. My bonus children are in their 20's now, but when I met my husband and they were pre-teens, it was a whole different story. At that time, I had to balance life in my home with my husband and the relationship we had with my bonus children.

To that end, we'll wrap up the great insight you have already received from the other sixteen Mommy Divas on the Move with me sharing a few tools of my own that will bless you whether you are a bonus mom or a single, divorced or widowed mom. I have learned via my own experience and through working with many of my clients in some bonus capacity that there are essential items needed in a Bonus Mommy's Tool Kit. Please allow me to share them with you.

B = Bonus Boundaries – I learned that discipline works most effectively when I allow my husband to discipline his kids. After all, they were with us for some time and with their mom for some time, and what we definitely wanted was for both homes to be in alignment as much as possible so the kids would feel at peace as they went between both homes. Although I could not manage what happened at their mom's, I could definitely manage the ease of their transition every time they came to stay with us. Now here's the big one. When my bonus kids were teens and we had an altercation, I would take these issues to my husband and we would discuss them together as a family. You must keep in mind that you may be well in your jurisdiction to reprimand your bonus kids while at your home, but if the kids are upset with you, they will take it to their mommy. And guess what happens after that? Turmoil in your home, and who has time for that? Having a family conversation allows for you to be a part of the conversation as they are disciplined and this helps them to understand the boundaries in YOUR home. Trust me, I have seen how it goes when there is no harmony, and you Mommy Divas are too busy for the added drama.

O – Be Open-minded – Be open-minded as you begin to build a relationship with your bonus children. You must keep in mind that you married your husband, not his kids, and it may take them some time to warm up to you. Allow your new bonus children to get to know you on their own terms. Don't force them to call you mom or do things for you on Mother's Day or anything like that. Carve out your own relationship with them in their own time and be open-minded as to what that looks like and how it unfolds. As I write this chapter, I have been together with my husband for ten years, married for seven, and just this past Mother's Day both of my bonus kids called me. Now my bonus son calls or texts me every year, but this year, my bonus daughter called, too. It always warms my heart to hear from them. My point is, relationships are built over time. Your bonus children will come around to you in their own time, if you give them the time and space to do so.

N = Nurture – As a bonus mom, it does help to nurture a relationship with the ex-wife, ex-girlfriend, etc. Yes, this is sometimes easier said than done, since in the beginning there may still be some hurt and resentment present. After all, they did break up for a reason, and you have to know some of that hurt and resentment can fall on you. But, don't take it personally. Have that smile on your face and let their ex know in your actions and in your words that you are there to support her and her children. I remember when I thanked my husband's ex-wife for allowing her children to be a part of my life. From that day forward, we have gotten along quite well.

U = Ultimatums are a NO-NO – I think my biggest lesson in being a bonus mom is summed up in this one sentence: *Keep in mind everything is not all about you.* Yes, we all can be divas in relationships…or maybe that's just me. (LAUGHS) However, you have to know that your husband may at times feel like he has to choose between you and his kids. To ease any tension, help him become comfortable with this as much as you can. Remind your mate that you always want what's best for your family. From the beginning of our relationship, I told my husband, "Your kids always come first." On the same token, make sure your bonus children feel like they take priority, just as you would for your own children. I remember when my husband and I were getting married. From the beginning when I met my bonus son, we instantly bonded. However, my bonus daughter was a different story. My bonus daughter, who is a daddy's girl, remained quiet and reserved around me for quite some time. Do you want to know how and when things shifted? Well, a few weeks before we got married, I pulled my bonus daughter to the side and said to her, "I want you to know that I know I will always be number two in your daddy's life." She said back to me, "Number two?" I said, "Yes, because YOU will always be number one." She smiled from ear to ear and gave me the biggest hug. I think that was the day we began our own relationship. It is your job to make sure everyone understands they don't have to choose between anyone to be in this relationship.

S = Support – Actively support your bonus children's relationship with their mom. It is not my job to tell them their mommy is wrong, even if I think she is. After all, she is their MOTHER, and it wouldn't be a good thing to contradict anything she says or does. All you can do is support them in making decisions that will help their relationship with their mom and your relationship with them. Additionally, it is equally important to nurture and support a relationship between your mate and his children. Because most men can become so focused on work, I have found it my job to make sure my husband stays connected with his kids. When I do, it builds up the support I get from his ex, as well. Lastly, don't exclude what is happening at their mom's house in the conversation in your home. They may have other siblings and cousins they may want to talk about. So, make sure your bonus children feel comfortable in your home and not like they have to cut off one part of their lives because they are currently with you.

So what does all of that have to do with being one of many Mommy Divas on the Move? This is yet an added layer to your hustle. By day, you may be making business deals, running meetings in boardrooms, and managing your business, but at night, you are handling the most important work of your life as you focus on your family. If your family is in chaos, you may have the tendency to channel that chaos into your career, allowing it to become part of your life. Even if you are on the other end of the continuum and dealing with a bonus mommy, girlfriend, etc. who is now with your ex, for the sake of your children, look at how you can take my tools and use them to your benefit. After all, it's all about your children being lifted up, nurtured, and cared for. Yes, the man who was once the love of your life is still the father of your children, and the smoother you make things at home, the smoother your life will be as one of the Mommy Divas on the Move.

The biggest tip I have for you as a Mommy Diva is to let go of your guilt or feelings of failure. You are not a perfect woman, so you will definitely not be a perfect mom. As a woman who has coached thousands of moms and as a bonus mom myself, I know this can be a difficult subject. I have to tell you that guilt and feelings of failure really come down to the negative conversation you have in your head about you. Think about it. How do you talk to yourself about what is happening in and around you on any given day? Do you say things like, "I can't believe you did that," "You are always late," or "When will you get your stuff together?" These or any statements of the like are negative conversations you have with you, about you, in your head.

This conversation reminds me of my client Kate. She text me one Saturday afternoon, and when I called her back, I could hear her sobbing on the other end of the phone. When I asked her what was wrong, she said, "I could hear your voice in my head all morning. So, although I felt guilty, I decided to take time for myself today and go out to brunch with my girlfriends. Well, during the entire brunch, I could not shake feeling guilty. I especially felt guilty because I know I'm going out of town tomorrow on business and have not spent any time with my son. So, when I got in the car, I called him immediately. My husband was picking him up from his friend's birthday party. Well, when my husband put my son on the phone, he sounded happy as he said, 'Mommy, I'm so glad you got to hang out with your friends today. I got to hang out with my friends, too, and now you, me, and Daddy get to have dinner together'. In that moment, I realized my son was fine. The guilt was just a story I'd been making up about not spending enough time with my son and feeling as though I was not being a good enough mom, just like the exercise you gave in our last session."

I am happy to tell you after that call and our three monthly sessions of working together, Kate not only learned to let go of that story she was telling herself, she is now standing in her power as both a mother and a mogul. She has built a beautiful relationship with her son and an even stronger partnership of love and mutual support with her husband. She designed a wonderful village of love, assistance, and encouragement. So much so that she has even started another business. All of this is because she obtained the tools needed to let go of the story she was telling herself of not being a good enough mom, which really was holding her back from fully standing in her power as a mom and an entrepreneur. I am really proud of Kate, what she has created, the money she is earning, the relationships she has designed, and most importantly I am proud to be her coach.

I mentioned my client Kate because some of you are just like her. Not every situation is the same, but you are looking for how to truly stand in your power as a mother and a mogul. So, I must ask you, what story are you telling yourself about not being a good enough mother? The best way to work through these emotions of guilt or feelings of failure is to look at the story you are telling yourself about doing something wrong or not being a good enough mom. When you tell yourself that story, I want you to ask yourself if you are really a bad mom or just an imperfect person?

If you are struggling with this, then that is why I'm here! It is because of women just like you that I became a coach. So I could serve you toward living in your full power in every role you play in your life. The thing I know for sure is that we have to be willing to be real with ourselves and fight to let go of the stories we tell ourselves as we learn how to embrace our brilliance and our breakdown. We must learn to accept that we will be fabulous and have slipups. It is just who we ALL are. So, know that you will not be all things to all people, nor should you be. Instead, strive for excellence and be the best you can be to each and every person in your life. Then get the support YOU need to juggle every ball you have going. After all, it is that support and village that will help you to be able to have it all and do it all. So, find the space to let go of the story you tell yourself that you are not good enough, the guilt of not doing it all, and allow yourself to stand in the authenticity of the fabulousness you already are as a mommy, an entrepreneur, a mogul, a wife or a mate, a sista friend, a sibling, a daughter, and every other role you play in your life. Find harmony and peace in knowing you are at your best and that is everything you need to be!

Throughout the course of this book, sixteen Mommy Divas have shared with you their stories of how they have learned to manage it all to have it all. Patrice has pulled together a great group of diverse women who are a part of the Mommy Divas on the Move-ment, and what I do know is that being a mompreneur is worth the struggle. I now hope that after reading *Mommy Divas on the Move* you know you can do it, too. One thing I hope you take away from our journeys is that it does take a village to raise a child. So, as a mommy, please reach out and ask for help. This book has started a movement, so be sure to reach out to Patrice to become a GLAMbassador for Mommy Divas on the Move in your area to create the support, encouragement, fellowship, and sisterhood that you need. Remember, it does take a village, so find your village to love and support your journey.

## *About the Author*

# PATRICE TARTT

Patrice Tartt is known as the hybrid of resiliency and passion topped off with a cherry-on-top ambition. As the ultimate Activator, she is a guru at turning what seems to be a nightmare into a dream and a dream into reality. She is the Founder and CEO of Patrice Tartt Publishing, LLC and Mommy Divas on the Move, LLC. In addition, she is a Speaker, Networking Virtuoso, and Coach for women and young girls. As a graduate of both Fisk University and Trevecca Nazarene University, Patrice has always been motivated to reach higher levels while simultaneously motivating others to do the same. After dealing with the unexpected death of her father in 2011, Patrice was led to seek therapy through writing. Unknowingly, Patrice's therapeutic writing sessions led to the completion of her debut novel *Wounds of Deception,* which allowed her to tell a tangled story of hurt, anger, and confusion.

The Milwaukee, Wisconsin native has a gift for connecting with other like-minded individuals, and in late 2013, she birthed the idea for the upcoming book collaboration and company *Mommy Divas on the Move*™ *of which she* is the Chief Mommy Diva. Patrice loves coaching women through her signature program that caters to women looking to become an entrepreneur. She also coaches young girls on how to write a book through her premier writing enrichment program, Girls Write Too™, offered through her publishing company. With a creative twist, she has the desire to educate and entertain through writing.

Patrice was a guest on *The Dr. Oz Show* and has been featured on several Blog Talk radio shows, in *Essence Magazine*, *The Network Journal*, Examiner.com, and SheKnows.com. Patrice is an active member of Alpha Kappa Alpha Sorority, Incorporated and supporter of the Amyloidosis Foundation in which she advocates and raises awareness for this rare disease addressed in her novel written in loving memory of her father.

Patrice currently resides in the Washington, D.C. area with her family and young son. In addition to writing, Patrice loves to travel, network, spend time with her family, and brainstorm ideas for the next best project. She is a dream chaser and the true meaning of a child of God who is living out her purpose and destiny.

For more information on the author, please visit her website and social media pages to stay connected and updated on new projects:

www.PatriceTartt.com
www.MommyDivasOnTheMove.com

Twitter: PatriceTartt & MommyDivasOTM
Facebook: Patrice Tartt & Mommy Divas On The Move
Instagram: PatriceTartt

# About the Co-authors

## Zelda Corona

Zelda Corona is an energetic individual who brings enormous vision and enthusiasm to any endeavor. As an Activator, she naturally makes things happen. Her passion is to motivate others to reach for the *unattainable* by teaching them how to change concept into reality. Corona holds a Bachelor of Arts Degree in Health Care Management and a MBA with an emphasis in Corporate Communication. As a Business Coach under her company Victory Vision Business Ventures, LLC, Zelda has created measurable strategies to stop self sabotaging behaviors in their tracks. Zelda also co-wrote the book *No Artificial Ingredients – Reflections Unplugged*, and she writes inspirational prose for a community newspaper. Corona has been featured on *NBC Today Miami, The Real Milwaukee Morning Show*, and other various news and radio appearances. Zelda believes in being one hundred percent responsible for her destiny, as she refuses to be a victim of any circumstance.

## Vicki Irvin

After building her first company into a million-dollar business in only twelve months, Vicki Irvin started her next venture coaching and mentoring business owners. Her focus is on teaching women how to have it all in Business, Beauty & Balance while living a "Superwoman Lifestyle".

Irvin has coached over 2,000 people on how to increase their wealth, boost their profits, and employ marketing strategies that few have been exposed to. The success of Vicki's coaching practice was built on her keen sense of marketing that keeps her events selling out in any economy. Vicki has been featured in *Millionaire Blueprint Magazine, USA Today, Essence Magazine,* and on *CNN's HLN Prime News, Lifetime TV, Bloomberg Radio, Essence.com, Investor's Business Daily,* and *Leading Experts.* Vicki is also the author of *The Superwoman Lifestyle Blueprint* and *The Secret Diary of a Superwoman,* which are both available on Amazon.

## Vikki Kennedy Johnson

Vikki Kennedy Johnson is a Soul Wealth mentor, living kidney donor, media executive, and proud mom. Her daughter is her inspiration for living a life of impact. A thought-provoking speaker, Vikki has influenced thousands of women over the last twenty years and has been featured as a keynote speaker for TEDx Women, The Pentagon, Department of Commerce, women's conferences, retreats, and workshops. *Coaching with Elder Vikki* supports women in transition, providing soul clarity and insight for their life vision. Her passion is to support women through the power of SistHERhood. Her signature brand, GIRL TALK UNPLUGGED, includes a bi-annual *"Ultimate Getaway Experience"*, *"Sacred SistHERhood Community"*, and *"Soul, Sun & Spa Luxury Weekend."* She has been the Pastor of Women at Kingdom Worship Center in Towson, Maryland since 1999. A bestselling author, her most recent book titled *Vikki-isms* is a collection of daily inspirations. She is a member of Delta Sigma Theta Sorority, Inc.

## Monikah Ogando

Monikah Ogando is CEO of the award-winning firm CEO Mastery, whose purpose is to equip organizations to become self-managing companies. With a unique blend of expertise in marketing, sales, strategy, and multi-media technology, CEO Mastery guides their clients through a support system to transform their business and quality of life. Monikah took her first company to rank as one of Inc. 500's fastest growing companies in the United States. She is an award-winning author and keynote speaker in the areas of leadership, marketing, and communication.

With a background in finance, Dr. Ogando has become an authority in building sustainable, leveraged, and profitable businesses. Her work has been featured on ABC, NBC, Fox, and CBS, and in *Entrepreneur Magazine*, *Inc. Magazine*, *U.S. News and Money*, *The Sun Sentinel*, and the *Miami Herald*. Dr. Monikah Ogando is the author of *On Fire: Seven Strategies to Ignite Your Business and Light Up Your Life*.

## Alea Anderson

With southern charm and an eclectic flare, Alea Anderson is an innovative influence who is directed by faith and leads by example. Her ability to persevere empowered her to pursue her BS in Fine Arts from Fisk University, and she presents a Masters prepared from Savannah College of Art and Design. She has been the ambassador for many schools and communities by educating young audiences through *Arts for Learning* and partnering with Fulton County Arts Council. Alea's talents have granted her many opportunities, as her work is displayed at Dunbar Park–Atlanta Georgia, Fisk University–Nashville, Tennessee, and owned by various private collectors across the country. Anderson's passion for creativity led her to establish Allure Designs, where she specializes in interior design and fine art. Alea is propelling her vision, as she has demonstrated the strength and dedication to say yes to her life's purpose while continuing to be obedient to her motto, "With God, YOU CAN!"

## Ayisha Hayes-Taylor

Ayisha Hayes-Taylor is a refreshing, powerful voice of resilience and hope for today's women. Passionate to see women awaken to launch their dreams, Ayisha has traveled the U.S. speaking at conferences, retreats, and workshops. Determined to provide the spark to ignite women to take action, she founded Lady Mogul Enterprise, a personal project administration company designed to help "mompreneurs" launch and elevate their small businesses. She co-authored the book *No Artificial Ingredients – Reflections Unplugged* and has been featured on *NBC Today Miami*, *The Real Milwaukee Morning Show*, and hosted a top-rated radio show on the Stellar Award-winning station 104.7 FM. In addition to writing, speaking, and running a successful company, she is a dedicated mother and wife. A mother of two, one with special needs, Ayisha is relentless in her fight to recover her son from Autism while providing hope to other families.

## Joan Thompson Wilson

Joan Thompson Wilson is an author of the Amazon.com bestseller *Don't Count Me Out: I'm Just Getting Started* and founder of the Corner Woman Movement for women who seek accountability and support to move past life's most difficult transitions. As a widow and a fighter of kidney disease, her unique talent is a "Let's Win" attitude, using her *Be A Knock Out*™ strategy approach which encourages women to not throw in the towel or count themselves out.

Joan helps women stand when they can't. In the midst of chaos or just life happening too fast, she helps women spar with adversity and box out fear, while gaining more confidence to condition their mindset to get it done. She is that voice from the corners of your mind. Joan is deeply committed to stepping in the mindset ring of your life and helping map out achievable strategies to win.

## Rhonda Wilkins

Rhonda Wilkins, a twenty-plus year veteran in the entertainment industry, is CEO of Atlanta-based event marketing and production boutique, Divas Unlimited, Inc., that has been featured in numerous national media outlets. Mrs. Wilkins is best known as the Creator and Executive Producer of the two annual award galas, *The Legendary Awards*, benefiting the newly formed Legendary Awards Foundation, and *The InfluenceHER Awards*, benefiting the March for Babies Campaign.

Wilkins serves as Executive Director for Glam Concierge, The Booking Agency, which is an Atlanta-based booking service for backstage productions of Fashion, Film, and Music industry events. Recognized as one of Atlanta's Top 100 Black Women of Influence, she also received The Women of Influence Award from WEDA and was inducted into the 14th Edition of Who's Who in Black Atlanta. Her work has been featured on BET, VH1, TV ONE, and BRAVO, as well as *in JET Magazine, SISTER 2 SISTER,* and *UPSCALE JEZEBEL.*

# Denise J. Hart

Denise J. Hart is wildly passionate about helping women live an Unapologetically Bodacious life and get laser focused on what's next in their life and business. She's a lively dynamic speaker, delivering her message with a touch of humor and a dose of "kick in the pants" honesty. She is committed to helping women become powerful confident speakers who are able to impact and influence in any speaking engagement.

Denise is a master at helping entrepreneurs identify the remarkable factor in their brand and is widely respected for her ability to help her clients increase sales by fifty percent within ninety days. She is a member of world renowned speaker Lisa Nichols' Global Leaders Team, a featured columnist at ForHarriet.com, and has written for *iCoach Magazine* and Girlfriendology.com. Her son Julian remains her inspiration to live an authentic empowered life.

# Kim Fuller

Kim Fuller is founder and CEO of Fuller Life Concepts, Inc., a company committed to empowering women, especially solo moms, around the world to discover, explore, learn, visualize, and embrace how they can create A Fuller Life. Kim is a Certified Professional Life Coach and Licensed Marriage and Family Therapist. Through her workshops, courses, coaching programs, and products, women learn to live life on their terms. She believes A Fuller Life is Possible.

As host of her radio show *Change Is Personal*, Kim focuses on educational and inspirational topics to help working moms go from feeling overwhelmed to being empowered.

Kim has been featured in *Balanced Mom Magazine*, was National Association for Professional Women 2013/14 Woman of the Year, was one of ten finalists in the Mom Entrepreneur of the Year contest, and is a contributing author in *Careers from the Kitchen Table 3rd Edition*.

## LeShawnda Fitzgerald

LeShawnda Fitzgerald is a passionate mother of two and creative entrepreneur who brings excellence and new vision in all pursuits. She is a compassionate teacher that helps students not only learn difficult subject matter, but gain a greater understanding of who they are as a person.

Through LeShawnda's innovation, she founded Ready For Spanish, a program that enhances children and adult's knowledge of the Spanish language and culture. She has created numerous educational materials for corporate America and many educational settings.

As a result of her expertise in various subjects, she has hosted workshops and speaks often on topics related to education, entrepreneurship, motherhood, and empowerment. She holds a Bachelors Degree in Spanish and History as well as Master Degrees in Education and English. In her spare time, she enjoys spending time with her children, is an active foster parent, and mentors to children within her community.

## Jennifer Fontanilla

Jennifer Fontanilla is a creative and driven entrepreneur constantly seeking ways to empower other individuals. A true renaissance woman, she is passionate about educating the community on things that were not taught in school, particularly finance and life skills. Jennifer is a financial coach and has designed several workshops and seminars that focus on taking action and the necessary steps to reach financial prosperity. Her clients have described her as approachable and excellent at explaining complex concepts in an easy way.

Jennifer has been featured in the national publication *Asian Enterprise* as well as receiving the *"Professional Woman of the Year 2011"* from The National Association of Professional Women. She continues to be a guest on local radio and TV shows, as well as a contributor sharing information on investments and insurance. Jennifer embraces challenges and believes they are given to you to prepare you for bigger things to come.

# Kiana Shaw

Kiana Shaw is the Founder/Executive Director of Village of Truth Inc., a non-profit organization that focuses on the wellbeing of teen girls. As a Prevention and Early Intervention Specialist, her mission is to provide abundant opportunities and the necessary resources for young girls to obtain financial stability, endure mental growth, enhance physical health, and acquire other much-needed life skills.

Kiana is also the founder and CEO of LeadHERshipAcademy.org, an online coaching site for women twenty-five to forty years old. She coaches women in life and business, connects them with the right people to forge their lives forward, and gives them the courage to do what is essential for further growth.

With a personal life motto of *Vision + Action = Elevation*, Kiana has positioned herself as an authority on teen and women's issues.

# Juanita Aguerrebere

Juanita Aguerrebere is a leading branding expert for Personal and Lifestyle Brands. Her mission is to work with global leaders and entrepreneurs as they collectively make a positive change in the world. She owns Innovative Internet & Media Solutions, LLC, a boutique web consulting company based in Honolulu, Hawaii. She has worked for over eight years behind the scenes with clients and supporting her tribe to launch brands globally.

Juanita is a mother of four kids, Samantha, Blaise, Antonio Joaquin, and Pancho. She is also the co-owner and founder of Aquahunters, a kayak fishing sports league, with Isaac Brumaghim. When Juanita is not slaying big ahi off her kayak with her boys, you can find her at yoga, reading, and surfing in her spare time. Juanita invites you to learn the secrets she has used with her clients to leverage their networks across the globe.

## Tiffany Bethea

Tiffany Bethea is a remarkable speaker, author, and mompreneur who is improving businesses and enriching lives with her infectious passion for growth and vitality. As the Spirit-Soul-Business™ Coach, she is assisting entrepreneurs everywhere with holistic business growth. After spending years behind the scenes building several faith-based brands, she stepped out into the forefront to serve the world in a larger capacity. Her education and experience have magnetically attracted her main clientele, which consists of small business owners, ministries/churches, authors, speakers, and entrepreneurs whose businesses are tied to serving the world. Tiffany is also the Founder & CEO of The L.I.V.E. Circle, a community designed to inspire, equip, and connect single mothers to their whole, flourishing, and fulfilled lives. Passionate, infectious, creative, and high-spirited, Tiffany's energy touches all those she comes in contact with. It is impossible to interact with her and not be ignited and stirred to take action and GROW.

## Avonti Garrett

Avonti Garrett is first and foremost a God-fearing woman with an assignment to save lives and recruit God's children. Through her trials and tribulations, God has taught her the utmost faith and has given her the wisdom and strength to endure.

Avonti was married to the late Grammy Award-winning singer and songwriter, Stephen "Static Major" Garrett, and they have three children. While his star was brightly shining, his life was unexpectedly taken at the age of thirty-three due to medical negligence. While grieving, Avonti was given several visions from God, visions that would save a lost generation. She decided to turn her pain into her passion and founded the Stephen Garrett School of Arts and the To Save a Life Foundation.

Avonti is completely devoted to providing outlets and mentorship to our at-risk youth. Avonti Garrett is a hardworker, and her light and spirt is truly a gift from God.

# Cheryl Wood

Cheryl Wood is a passionate and energetic motivational speaker and business coach who possesses a deep rooted passion for supporting the personal development and economic empowerment of women globally. Cheryl has impacted the lives of thousands of women through her life-changing principles of FEARLESS living. She is an award-winning entrepreneur, speaker, and author who specializes in equipping women to stretch their expectations and play bigger. Her message of empowerment has been spotlighted on *Fox 5 News, News Channel 8*, Radio One, WPGC, WHUR, My Spirit DC and *Afro-American Newspaper*, to name just a few.

Made in the USA
Charleston, SC
15 December 2014